About Island Press

Since 1984, the nonprofit organization Island Press has been stimulating, shaping, and communicating ideas that are essential for solving environmental problems worldwide. With more than 1,000 titles in print and some 30 new releases each year, we are the nation's leading publisher on environmental issues. We identify innovative thinkers and emerging trends in the environmental field. We work with world-renowned experts and authors to develop cross-disciplinary solutions to environmental challenges.

Island Press designs and executes educational campaigns, in conjunction with our authors, to communicate their critical messages in print, in person, and online using the latest technologies, innovative programs, and the media. Our goal is to reach targeted audiences—scientists, policy makers, environmental advocates, urban planners, the media, and concerned citizens—with information that can be used to create the framework for long-term ecological health and human well-being.

Island Press gratefully acknowledges major support from The Bobolink Foundation, The Curtis and Edith Munson Foundation, The Forrest C. and Frances H. Lattner Foundation, The Freedom Together Foundation, The Kresge Foundation, The Summit Charitable Foundation, Inc., and many other generous organizations and individuals.

The opinions expressed in this book are those of the author(s) and do not necessarily reflect the views of our supporters.

Barn Gothic

Barn Gothic

THREE GENERATIONS AND THE
DEATH OF THE FAMILY DAIRY FARM

Ryan Dennis

◖ **ISLAND**PRESS | Washington | Covelo

Library of Congress Control Number: 2025937937

All Island Press books are printed on environmentally responsible materials.

Manufactured in the United States of America
10 9 8 7 6 5 4 3 2 1

The author received financial support from the Arts Council of Ireland in the creation of this work.

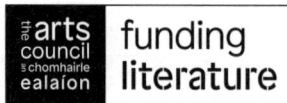

Keywords: agribusiness; American agriculture; American Farm Bureau Federation; dairy industry; displaced generation; Farm Bill; farm debt; farm economics; farm memoir; farm succession; fathers and sons; food production; food security; milk prices; multigenerational farm; New York dairy farming; rural America; working-class families

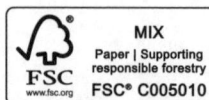

To my family and families like them

Contents

Prologue

"LOOK AT ALL THAT COLOR," my father said. He took a large swig from his mason jar and cleared his throat, readying himself for the conversation ahead. His small, motley beef herd moved along the sidehill, grazing.

Our neighbors, other dairy farmers who had sold out, bought starter herds of Angus or Herefords. My father had a few Milking Shorthorns and a handful of Holsteins still on the farm. He bred them to beef and kept them in the freestalls. The next generation was less a beef herd than a miscellany of brown, mahogany, and black. It did, however, give my father chores to do every morning between bus runs. He enjoyed watching the cows slowly work their way along the horizon while he sat on the front porch. He liked going to the pasture to see who had calved.

A few years before, my parents went to the market to buy a Black Angus bull for the first time. After they returned home, they were dismayed to find a white spot on its forehead.

"They move the cattle through the ring so fast," my father said.

My mother tried to defend him. "Maybe they put some manure on it to cover it up."

Most of what was born the next year was black and white. The farm once again had Holstein calves running around.

"So what do you want to know?" my father asked. His voice was deeper than usual. He sank back, stretched his legs, and stared ahead. He wasn't reticent or gruff, nor did he fit any of the other stereotypes of farmers. Instead, he shaved every day and dressed well in public, always in an open button-down over a T-shirt and a brown Syracuse Orangemen hat. The mason jar in his hand was left over from a winter, long ago, when my mother thought she would try canning. It was full of water and gin.

At first, I was surprised that my father would talk about what had happened. However, he clutched the jar, steeling himself against the memories. My father was from the last generation of farmers to be told they were the backbone of the nation. Government policy encouraged low milk prices, which allowed manufacturers and retailers to prosper—but not farmers. Part of what my father lived through was a failing industry, and part of it was what that does to people.

Even though it was summer, the porch had firewood stacked under the eaves. In New York State there is no way to know when the last cold day will be, and so no one thinks to carry the remaining chunks back to the pile at the end of the lawn. Because we tended to split the wood in front of the porch, often only as it was needed, the lawn was littered with splinters and the holes the dog made whenever it heard the axe hit the timber, giving in to a strange compulsion. Also on the front porch was a grill that my father used all year round, going onto the concrete in his socks with a spatula in his hand, because he usually cooked in our family. There were tools from various projects left around us, as well as toys from my sister's children. We saw these objects every day but no longer realized they were there.

My father sat in a wooden rocking chair with handles the dog had chewed on. I sat in another one. My mother had probably found them both at a yard sale. I drank my gin out of a coffee mug, straight.

I was in my mid-thirties and thought I had a sense of how to lead an interview, even if it was with my own father. I asked him about the dairy industry in America and all the changes he had seen in his lifetime. I figured it was best to get him talking comfortably first, even if it wasn't what I was after. For all the conversations in the past where I knew I was supposed to say something to him but didn't know how to do it, at least this time I had a script.

Also, however, the question wasn't disingenuous. A lot about farming had changed, and that had consequences. Between 2002 and 2019, the United States lost over half of its dairy herds. Agribusiness grew quickly, but during these years the average dairy farm only made a profit twice. As a result, a whole subculture of America disappeared in two decades. It was a quiet violence that affected tens of thousands of families, and no one outside of these households seemed to be talking about it. My father never said this, but I think he would agree: Those who make up that statistic have the right to see what happened written down, and they deserve for everyone else to see it, too.

"I don't miss it," my father said, suddenly. "I don't miss it. There's a new chapter in my life." He took another swallow and set the glass on the concrete. "I've moved on."

As a school bus driver, my father thrived being around people. For the first time he was in the public and had an audience for his wit. He had time to visit friends and go places. Every summer he invited the staff at the bus garage to our pond. The year after he quit dairy farming, my parents went to the Grand Canyon. Still, this wasn't the first time he said that he didn't miss milking cows. At first, I thought he was trying to convince himself. Until then, dairy farming had been everything he had done. However, later I started to wonder if he wasn't saying it for my sake instead. Maybe he didn't want me to question the choices I had made.

I knew, without asking, that my father couldn't have moved on. He drove bus because he still had debt to pay. The rhythms of farming—of dairy farming, specifically—stay inside a person long after the last cow is milked, telling them when to feed, when to start the night milking, when to get up in the morning, and all the time reminding them that they're not farming. More troubling, the organs on the right side of his body bulged out of his torn abdomen and he had a metal rod in his back. Every movement hurt him, and it got worse every year. He refused the lifetime prescription of painkillers the doctor had given him, but increasingly self-medicated with gin towards the evening so that he could fall asleep for at least a few hours. While my father said that he had moved on, he carried the pain of the dairy industry with him wherever he went.

At one point, when the time was right, I asked about the story of our farm. He knew what I meant. Because a farm is its own center of gravity, it determines how the people on it live and die.

Every farm has two histories. One is the version given to visitors, whether 4-H'ers, members of an FFA club, or distant cousins dropping by. It is sanitized, protective, and delivered in bullet points. It includes what changes were made on the farm and when, and how many cows were milked at the time. Occasionally, while leaning forward on his knees, my father answered questions like he was being profiled in a farming magazine. He made grand statements about how the registered cow business "piqued a farmer's interest" and how there was a time when the harder a person worked, the more money they got. He talked about how the way farmers fed cows changed through the years and the difference in having hill ground. Eventually, though, he gave me the second story: what happens to people on a farm when that farm struggles.

The sounds of the cattle chewing above us made the type of white noise that the evening could settle into. The dog sauntered by, and my father grabbed it and patted its ribs briskly. He was probably glad to give his hands something to do. The dog was a rescue Aussie my parents had gotten a few years earlier. The dog half-yawned, its teeth grinning.

My father was, above all, a man of stories. There were times he had little else, so he knew the value they had. Our story, as he saw it, was the gift I asked for. In offering it, he showed that he believed in my ambitions as a writer and the decisions I had made, despite what it cost him. Maybe he thought I could get the story right.

My father's eyes grew watery as he stared into the past again. At one point he pulled the top of his shirt up to rub his cheeks.

Whenever I returned home, my father set my boots out on the corner of the porch. The first few days I dwelled too much on small assurances. I enjoyed seeing again how big the two walnut trees were in the lawn. They were at least two hundred years old, and at that size looked the same as they always had. I appreciated all the birdsong that surrounded our family's house. I had never realized it was there until I first left for college. I have traveled much since then and never came across anything similar. I mentioned the birds to my parents every time I came back.

"What about Grandpa?" I said. "Do you regret anything?"

"Just a second. You probably need a refill too."

I handed him my mug. What I didn't have the courage to say was, *What about us?*

The sound of the faucet came through the open window behind me. Because I'd seen it before, I knew that the water foamed at the top of the jar once it was filled, already having gin in it. If my father had a lime he would use it, but usually he didn't. He screwed a cap closed. Then he came back onto the porch and handed me the mug and lowered himself into his chair again.

He sat there for a long time. A red squirrel ran up the walnut tree in front of us. It moved in short bursts and then froze, its nails clicking against the bark. The cattle had started to circle, which meant that was probably where they would bed down. A car passed, but neither of us looked to see if the person waved.

"Just make it a happy story," my father said.

I.
A Childhood Closing

Cows Do Not Dream

Mʏ ʙᴏᴏᴛs ʟᴀʏ ғʟᴀᴛ ᴜɴᴅᴇʀ ᴛʜᴇ ᴘᴏʀᴄʜ ʟɪɢʜᴛ, kicked off the night before. The duct tape used to patch them flickered when the wind blew. I slipped them on, dried manure shattering over the ground, and followed my father into the morning darkness.

The dry cow pasture started at the edge of the lawn and beyond that, fields and hedgerows sloped into a gully. At that hour, nothing stirred in the valley. We were solitary creatures trudging towards the barn, my smaller shadow behind his larger one. Our boots scraped the worn path from the porch to the milk house in the same strides, knocking the dew off the grass around us. I was in my early teens, but I too brought a cup of coffee that spilled over the sides.

We tapped the end of the stalls to stir the cows to their feet. Cows do not dream but wait patiently for someone to compel them towards the parlor. Only one ceiling light worked, and it put everything below it in a filmy haze. The rafters were high and the lights in them were wider than what a man could put his arms around. The company that installed them did not know farming or what it would become: that if a farmer could not fix something himself then it would not get fixed. My father, though, did change one bulb. To reach it, he extended the bucket of the loader tractor to its limit and climbed it with his tallest ladder. The only thing that kept the ladder in place was the smooth slope of the bucket as my father dragged the heavy light up the rungs. The fact that the ladder held and my father did not lose his balance was a quiet miracle, one of the many that sustained him each day.

The cows' hooves knocked against the concrete as the cows moved, and the things we shouted at them echoed under the tin roof. We yelled *come on* and *let's go* and sometime sang parts of country songs. My father called them beautiful bitches as he struck their thurls and pushed them towards the holding area. Sometimes a cow would not get up. She was either sick or not, but it didn't matter. It is the same for both the cow and the farmer: Once you cannot stand, you are dead, and until then you must keep moving. That cow would be hit. The most stubborn of cows would shake their ears and snort and take the beating. Eventually, though, the cow would rise because she had to. She would be given calcium or made to swallow a magnet, and perhaps sent to the sick pen if that would help. And if she didn't need it, she would be called a bastard because we knew we would have to hit her again the next day.

In the holding area, cows stood in all angles and directions, like something that had to be put back together. They chewed their cuds and gazed at things we could not see. If the air was particularly cool, steam would rise off their backs in the darkness. Wash water crashed through the milkers that lined both sides of the parlor pit, shaking violently on their hooks. The floor was still damp from the last milking. We restacked the paper towels and filled the dippers with iodine and made sure the radio station was clear, although it was never turned off from the night before.

After the wash cycle, the vacuum pressure was flipped on, and a pulse ran through the parlor. I started at the first cow, dipping her teats in iodine, and then went to the next one. My father followed after me with brown paper towels, wiping the udders clean. His hands worked with a consciousness of their own and he did not have to look at nor think about the things he did. Iodine spilled over my fingers and splashed onto the front of my shirt when a cow kicked at me, and the bitter smell lasted the rest of the morning. Manure dried in the hair of our arms, but we did not pick it off. When we finished one row of cows, we went down the other and then slipped the teats into the milkers.

After all the milkers were on, we had a few moments to lean against the pipeline. The constant throb of the vacuum pressure filled the space between us. Those who don't know any better believe that the rhythm of farming is seasonal, going from plowing to planting to harvest, but that's only what people see from the road as they drive by. The real cadence is a daily one, as the morning moves from milking to feeding cows to feeding calves, fieldwork, and then milking and feeding again. Then another day. This rhythm is driven by the throb of the milkers, filling the chest and replacing the heartbeat.

When every cow had a milker hanging below her, I sat on the rusting steps and had the thoughts that a twelve- or thirteen- or fourteen-year-old would have. After it's over, a childhood is not chronological, but something pieced together over and over again to find what is needed. My father left to scrape the freestall alleys, since they didn't have any cattle in them. He pushed the manure towards the grates at the end of the barn with the skid-steer bucket. The shit is supposed to flow through the grates and slip into the manure lagoon, but a handful of years after the freestall barn was built, the tiles beneath the ground collapsed. Afterwards, he had to bucket the manure and dump it outside the barn. When it rained, cow shit stretched across the back driveway.

By the time he finished scraping, I had milked one, maybe two groups of cows and let them back inside the freestalls. He navigated the skid steer around them, sometimes tapping the back of their hocks gently with the end of the bucket to get them to move. A few years later, my father would be crushed by the arms of the skid steer in a freak accident that would break his back and tear apart his organs. He would use the last of his strength to drag himself through the manure in the alley until he made it to the parlor, where he waited to die alone. However, he did not know that yet on this morning, as he drove the skid steer up the lip of the concrete and spilled a little behind him. I did not know it, either, sitting on the parlor steps and watching the cows milk out, thinking that someday I would be a farmer, too.

My father and I passed the time by talking. He told me what fields he wanted me to plow that day and how to plow them. Because I couldn't interpret his directions, he would take a brown paper towel out of his back pocket and draw the shape of the field. His fingers ran up and down the paper in the direction I should drag the plows, lengthwise first, and then perpendicular for the headlands. He always remembered where the dead furrow was left last year. Afterwards, he'd tell me about a movie he watched and then, unable to help himself, explain the entire plot. It was often a zombie film. At first my father did not care for zombies, but he would inevitably take an interest in what I liked, if only to give us something to talk about in the parlor. We analyzed the starting rotation of the Chicago Cubs and thought about what the Bills would look like next season. Sometimes we repeated conversations we already had, and we both knew it, but we said it all again anyway.

The parlor's corners had cobwebs that didn't get washed away by the hose at the end of the milking. The walls yellowed with age; we nailed wooden boards over spots where the bull rubbed his head until he pushed it through. Iron dividers that separated the cows rusted and flaked, the debris collecting at the mouth of the drain. Once in a while, my father had to push a long rod along the duct to free the water.

There were things we didn't talk about. We didn't talk about bill collectors or the future of the farm. We never said out loud the things we were afraid of, and we didn't talk about what anything meant. He never mentioned emotions. We talked about my dreams and ambitions, but never his. My father never told me why we farmed. It must have been implied, because I never asked.

Once, I opened the parlor door and found my father sitting on a five-gallon feed pail with his head in his hands. At certain points during the milking, one of us might leave briefly to feed calves or get another cup of coffee, but the milking would continue. It had to, because the day turned on first getting the cows milked. That person would return and fall into the motion of dipping and wiping the teats, and then putting the milkers on. My father must have heard me enter, but he didn't look up. He never complained about the things he had to do and the ways he had to do them. He never let what farming had become show on his face, being the shield our family stood behind. Of the things to come in the years ahead, my father on that pail would remain one of the most heinous images of my childhood. There was nothing to say about what he must have been feeling, because we did not have names for such things.

I moved past him, to the end of the parlor, and climbed the steps to the holding area. I put my hand on the tailheads of the cows I passed, in a way that I could not put my hand on my father's shoulder. A heifer might startle and push into the animals in front of her, but most cows would shift their rear legs out of my way or ignore me entirely. There was a metal screen on the back wall, caked with manure, and I looked through it to the valley around us. The first light of the day cast our hill into pools of shadow. The trees along the hedgerows and the electric poles and the goldenrod in the ditch were still the shapes of things and not the things themselves. Perhaps that is what a childhood is, the chance to see the world at a remove before having to step into it. Nonetheless, the future awaiting my family and those like us would not stay abstract for long.

This Is the Picture on the Postcard

My father checked the tailgate of my grandfather's pickup and wiped away the dust, making the dents more apparent in the sunshine. There was a bolt sticking out at the loading dock of the feed store. "He backs into it every time," he told my mother. They laughed at getting old. We all kicked off our boots on the porch and went inside.

Breakfast at my grandparents' was a performance that was often the same, as if the regularity of farming also governed the life around it. My grandfather would start telling us about an article he had read in an agricultural journal and then suddenly walk to the bathroom, his arms swinging from hunched shoulders. He would then come back with the magazine folded to an inside page and point to the title. After he sat down someone would make an observation. "If it doesn't stop raining, we'll never get the corn in," or "Fuel jumped again—damn, it never stops." The remarks changed little. Farming, at that time, was the best it would ever be.

I always sat on a stool next to my grandmother. Because the metal legs were long, I had to lean down to reach my plate. I'd wear a pair of my grandfather's barn jeans, the waist folded over a few times. Mine were caked with manure and iodine and left on the bench in the back room. My father did the same, although his borrowed pair didn't quite fit him either. We ate buckwheat pancakes and breakfast sausage. My father and I put homemade peach jam and maple syrup on the sausage, even though my mother said that covering meat with sugar was a bad habit my grandmother had given us. My sister was on a stool, too, on the other side of my grandmother.

During these conversations, my grandmother would hold a stern face with one elbow on the table and occasionally open her palm, as if it held something to complement what the men were saying. She would offer, "How can they expect anyone to survive? The farmer is always going to take it down the throat," and follow that with, "The price of feed is crazy." Sometimes, if nearing the end of a topic or if my grandmother's complaint felt like a cadence, my grandfather would push both hands in front of him and conclude, "It's all just a game," or "We can never win." To this my father would nod, three times at least, and maybe four times.

My mother had to wedge her way into these conversations. She was college educated and worked both on and off the farm, either of which might have made my grandparents a little suspicious of her. She would not sit quietly, however. If she could not remark on the wetness of a particular field or the price of beef, she would introduce another topic. If my grandfather told how his brother hauled a load of Amish women to another part of the state in a cattle trailer to get impregnated, she would explain that it was because the Amish were genetically bottlenecked. If my father felt like he needed to intervene, he would say, "Well, they're good workers. They work hard."

In the small silences between discussions, we found ourselves staring out the window at my grandfather's farm, the view mostly the same over the years. Emily, our border collie, crouched in the back of our pickup. Whenever someone turned the key, she spun in circles and barked at the tires. Across the driveway, the loader tractor would be parked next to the calf hutches, its antennae flickering above it. A barn cat might be sitting on the front wheel, tucking itself between the tread and closing its eyes against the breeze. It would wrap its tail around its legs and pin its ears back, concentrating on its sleep. Empty teat dip drums were piled outside the milk house door. One of them might rock back and forth on its side when the wind caught it. The dirt underneath the tractor was stained from its air conditioner dripping. The tractor's bucket was raised high, poised.

Our family's history starts with a pond on top of a hill. It was first dug by my great-grandfather, Clair Dennis, as a watering hole for cattle during the Great Depression. He lived and milked there for two years without electricity. Because the milk carts, pulled by horses, could not make the climb, every day he hauled his milk down the hill in metal cans.

Since the hill was the highest point in the county, the wind tore over it in winter. Hunters and neighbors still sometimes talk about the gusts they meet there. When electric lines finally passed through the bottom of the valley, Clair moved to the home I grew up in. His final words as he left the pond may have been "Good riddance."

Clair didn't go far to find a wife. Beneath some brush, remains of an old stone foundation mark where my great-grandmother Esther was born. It is two hundred yards from the house Clair and Esther moved into. My grandfather, Andy, was born in their home forty-six years before I was. I have a few pictures of my grandfather and his siblings as children. The woodshed behind them eventually became our kitchen.

Andy married a redhead named Sharon and they moved to the northern part of New York State, where he worked as an artificial inseminator in the dairy industry. After only a year, Clair asked him to come back home. Esther had chronic emphysema and required more care, and Clair needed help building a new barn. My father was born in a house one hundred yards away, where Andy and Sharon lived. Clair and Andy were meant to farm together, but the father and son, as the story goes, couldn't get along. The details of how the agreement went bad are unknown by now and may never be discovered. Instead, Andy and Sharon bought the next farm over when it came up for sale.

When my father was still in high school, he took over Clair's farm and paid all the cousins their share. A hired hand milked in the morning and my father milked at night. Not long after graduating, he met my mother, the daughter of a German immigrant, at the bottom of the other side of the hill.

My grandfather, Andy, and my father, Rick, had separate herds but shared the land, the equipment, and the jokes about all the money they weren't making. Aunt Kelly lived in the house next to my grandfather's farm, and my grandfather later put a prefab next to the pond to retire in. On the border of Allegany and Steuben Counties in western New York State, there's a stretch of road that starts at the top of North Hill and extends over a mile. All told, it includes five houses in a row that all had Dennises in them one time or another. At one point, the land that we owned stretched even farther. In the end, there is a geography to our family. Because, like Clair, my father married a neighbor, much of the family on both sides is within two miles. Every Sunday with good weather we met at the pond to enjoy the breeze.

Everything we did was the continuation of something before us. We milked cows and fed calves because our parents and grandparents did these things. The Dennises pulled plows through the same piece of ground as the men in our family before them, and although the tractors and plows we used changed, the nature of how we farmed didn't. We put corn in the dirt in the spring and then chopped it in the fall. We cut hay and made silage in the summer. We speculated how other farms were doing. We did the predictable things we knew to do, like follow high school basketball teams, have family reunions, and drink Miller High Life after a day in the field. The Dennises grew up, married, and got old, all the while farming. It was bigger than all of us and something that couldn't be broken.

The morning my parents laughed at his tailgate was a few years after my grandfather's accident, which became one of the ways time was marked in our family. He had fallen in the milking parlor and hit his head on the concrete floor, but on this day, we might have still believed that he had recovered. I was sixteen or seventeen, but because there were still only four chairs, I had to sit on a stool. Our mouths tasted like syrup and jam. There was likely a crinkled farm journal next to my plate, creased to an article about tractor safety or judging cattle or something else that was supposed to make me a better farmer. The adults had already complained about the price of milk. I can't remember what the weather was like on this day, nor any other specific details, besides what happened next. However, my grandmother would have opened up her palm with a lament. My grandfather would have thrown up his hands and declared it all a game. My father would have nodded.

And then my grandmother turned to my grandfather with her hand on her forehead. "Andy, why is our tractor going down the road?"

My grandfather shrugged, put down his fork, and then seemed to realize the content of the question. He pushed himself out of his chair and staggered to the window, his knees snapping as he walked. My parents got up quickly and my sister and I hopped off our stools. We crowded together until we fit the width of the glass and could hear each other breathing. We stared down the cracking blacktop road that split our land in half. Our loader tractor went past us in high gear with the silhouette of someone we didn't know, in the direction of the John Deere dealership.

My father rushed to the back room and pulled his boots over his bunched-up pant legs. My grandfather's jeans sagged on him. He ran down the driveway, pumping his arms. He moved awkwardly, stepping on the flat part of his feet to keep the boots on, scraping over the gravel and kicking up dirt. He jumped into our truck and sped down the road, Emily dashing back and forth in the bed.

My grandfather returned to his chair and watched out the window. His elbows rested on the table, his fingers balled up. His arms had an old tan that darkened his skin and faded his age spots. His nose curved and his ears drooped loosely behind his hair, as if everything were being pulled towards the ground.

"I'm sure it's just a misunderstanding," my grandmother said, quietly.

My grandfather looked ahead with an empty stare.

We heard the heels of boots striking concrete on the porch and then saw them heaved into the lawn. The back door opened and snapped shut. My father walked into the kitchen, slammed a dirty toolbox on the counter, and sat down in his seat. He turned to my grandfather. "You didn't say you were four payments behind."

Everyone stared at the toolbox on the counter. Two rusty bolts stuck out of the back, one with a bent washer hanging on it, swinging quietly. Dust outlined two handprints where the box had been thrust off the frame of the tractor. It was soiled and left grease smudges on my grandmother's counter. The dangling washer rocked inside the bolt's thread and held the attention of our family.

A Trail of Gum Wrappers

AN OLD ROUND BALE HAD GROWN DARK sitting in the weeds of a hedge-row. It had probably been rained on before it was baled and wasn't needed that year. A red-tailed hawk landed on it and was tearing apart a frog.

The hawk shifted to watch me as I passed by, but never took flight. I was bent forward, gripping the steering wheel. I stared into the dirt in front of me, at the boundary between the ground that had been disked once and the ground that had been disked twice, trying to keep the front left tire parallel to that line. As the overturned ground dried in the sun, though, the border was sometimes hard to interpret through the dusty windows of the cab.

The plates of the disk rattled behind me. Because I was only thirteen, I went slow. Disking the plowed ground was one of the first types of fieldwork I was asked to do. I was in the tractor that would be repossessed a few years later, but I only knew that the ache from sitting in its cab all day made me an adult.

I looked up and found my grandfather at the edge of the field with the five-row planter. Its green paint and yellow seed boxes looked regal over the pale dirt around it. He slowly lowered the marking arm. Then he started planting corn. I was coming down the field and could watch him in front of me.

I was five when my grandfather and I stood at the base of his silo. He looked down at me and told me to never climb a silo with a wrench in my pocket. He said that it could fall out and kill someone on the ground. "I'm not giving you hell or anything," he said. "Just telling you." The silo was over eighty feet tall. I had no intention of climbing it, nor bringing a wrench.

The first time we passed by each other in the field, only a few disk-lengths away, he waved. This was before his accident. There was an overlay of friendliness to him that made him easy to be around, and that's how most people knew him to be. However, he was also deeply pragmatic. What he showed the world wasn't what he thought of it. Sometimes, if you watched him long enough and he didn't know it, you could see him making calculations.

In some fields, a red or blue handkerchief flickered inside a hedgerow. It would be tied to a branch along the edge of the dirt. When plowing or disking, especially if it was sod ground, the tractor operator got jostled in the seat all day. This could be hard on digestion. It was impractical to drive the machinery back home, even if one could make it in time. Instead, whenever my grandfather's intestines got upset, he went into the hedgerow or edge of the woods and then wiped with his handkerchief. When he was done, he tied it to a branch. The summer rains had cleaned it by the time the corn had to be chopped in the fall, so he took it home again.

I drew back on the throttle as I neared the end of the field. The engine noise lowered in pitch as the tractor slowed. Heat lifted off the hood and blurred everything around it. Sometimes dust built up on the outside of the windshield and then streaked down the glass. No matter what field-work we did, the pattern of doing it was the same: around the field four times and then up and down one side, turning around on the headlands that had already been worked. My grandfather had planted corn along the outside of the field. The fine marks left by the drills lineated the dirt. I had been told to go over the whole field twice. I turned around on the headlands as I had before, my wide disks pulling through the rows of planted seed.

My grandfather was hesitant about me doing fieldwork, fearing I would make a mistake that would be costly. My father told him that I had to learn somehow. I'm not sure if my father said that to me as a confidant, being the only other person standing in the field at that time, or to gently indicate how expensive mistakes with machinery could be. Usually, when my father disagreed with my grandfather it was in private. Only as an adult did I realize that it was sometimes on my behalf.

From what I can remember, Grandpa Dennis wasn't the type of grandfather to get down on the floor and play with children, nor entertain long conversations with them. He had lines he repeated as jokes, and the few times we were alone together he slipped into giving me advice on how to put an insulator on a fence post or a gate on a hinge. Not knowing how to spend time with children, he reverted to treating them like small adults. To compensate, though, he would play modest pranks. He might pretend to throw my sister and me into the pond at a picnic or put potatoes in our boots when he visited. For years, whenever we came to his house and walked into the living room, he would be standing around the corner, waiting to yell *boo*. He continued to jump from the corner, even into my early teens when I had to pretend to be surprised.

Instinctively, I wanted to emulate my grandfather. I wore a Pioneer Seed hat in the cab like him. The green fabric had white sweat crystals in the headband. I said "gawd" when I was exasperated and "sine" instead of "something" because that's how he talked. I carried a handkerchief in my back pocket. A few times I also tied it to a branch. He was the quintessential farmer, looking the part, and that's who I wanted to be. He chewed Wrigley's gum and ate York Peppermint Patties, and when I climbed into the tractor with him as a child, I'd finger them out of the cubby hole by the armrest. Years after he was gone, I sometimes found Wrigley's gum wrappers in the dirt I turned over while plowing.

For my grandfather there was farming and not farming, and that which was not farming was vague to him. He did what one might expect of a grandparent, going to the school concerts my sister and I were in, and sometimes to our basketball games. Once he sat in the stands during my first year of Little League. Afterwards, he told me that my team might have won if I had made the throw to home. It was hard to hear, but he wasn't wrong. Much later, at the age of twenty-five, I had a personal essay accepted in *Progressive Dairyman*. Agricultural magazines didn't usually publish creative work, but the editor had a literary background. My grandfather saw my name in one of the farming journals he had always read and was proud. "You keep doing what you're doing," he told me. "You just keep doing it."

I turned the tractor from the far headlands and started down the field again. The planter was stopped at the other end. My grandfather stood at the bottom of the steps with his hands on his hips. He looked at the ground and squinted. Because it took a while to reach the end of the field, I had plenty of time to watch him.

The Ford rocked back and forth after I pressed the clutch. I pulled the parking brake, climbed down, and met my grandfather between our equipment.

He looked into a distant hedgerow and then at me. "You disked where I had already planted. Now that corn won't grow."

He spoke evenly, without anger showing. It was only because I knew him that I could tell he was annoyed. Later, it seemed obvious that I should not take the disk over planted ground, even if I didn't get to disk that part a second time. Instead, I had followed the directions I had been given verbatim, a habit that would later haunt me.

"Well, now you know," my grandfather said, heading back towards his tractor.

When the past becomes history, it transitions into a set of facts that hold little emotion. Grandma Dennis's father died well before I was born. I knew he liked to read and fish, and that was all I needed to like him. On my mother's side, Grandpa Kramer's father was a lieutenant for the Germans in World War II. The family narrative was that he was forced into it to keep his wife and children safe. It doesn't matter if that is true or not. I have no bad feelings towards him because it is only a chronological detail. I never met him.

In the company of a child, everything is immediate. A person's prior life and the decisions made in it don't exist for them. Grandchildren want to admire their grandparents. They're made that way. While the past doesn't matter to them, however, sometimes the future is more complicated.

Night Sets on a Wild Dry Cow

WE MET AT THE TIN BARN AFTER EVENING CHORES. The heifers and dry cows stood by the feeder wagon in the last light of a summer evening and watched us. We threw our gloves on the seat of the tractor and started moving gates. My grandfather had driven the John Deere there, but my father and I had walked. Around us the distant shadows of gray squirrels wove through brush and undergrowth as they headed towards their nests. After the usual greetings, no one spoke. The right moment to talk would be later, once the dry cow was inside and we could put a boot on the hitch or lean on the back of the trailer. Then we could tell about our day for a few minutes before heading off. Now, we tied gates together with chain until it ran out and then used twine.

Because there were three of us, it meant that my father knew this dry cow would be difficult to separate and bring home. There were probably only a few days before she would have a calf and return to the freestalls. Most cattle mellow with age. They begin to understand what is put before them, which is to calve, to milk, and to dry off before freshening again. Still, every once in a while, there was a cow that railed against this agreement.

The cow stopped chewing her cud when the gate opened. She was a deep-barreled Holstein, probably on her third or fourth calf. Her eyes were already wide and flighty. No sooner had my father pointed her out that she alighted with the rest of the heifers and dry cows towards the end of the pasture, pushing herself into the middle of the herd.

In summer I wore shorts with barn boots. Cow shit often clung to my legs and the hair was rubbed off my shins. A few days into the warm weather I stopped noticing the rubber slapping on my bare skin. My father lifted the last gate while my grandfather slotted its pins into the hinges of the previous one. Then my father swung it open. The channel the gates created narrowed towards the trailer. The three of us headed into the pasture. In the silence I heard my boots again.

The tin barn was down the road from where we kept our other non-milking stock. It stood at the beginning of a large gully between my father's and my grandfather's farms. When the leaves changed, the colors set the type of background found on postcards and paintings. Often the cattle there watched us walk into the gully with shotguns during deer season, turning their heads in unison as we passed. Some would follow and then put their necks over the wire and stare at our backs until we were gone. Because we were inside the fence this time, however, they knew we were coming for one of them.

We reached the back of the pasture and allowed the cattle to bend around us, putting the herd between us and the trailer. The cattle trotted ahead and then eventually turned as they neared the barn. Part of knowing cattle is using angles to make them move in the right way, and we winnowed out the animals around the dry cow and allowed them to scamper past. Whenever the dry cow turned, whoever was closest to her put up his hands and shouted. It was muddy near the barn from cattle traffic. It gripped at our feet and made our steps heavy. Often someone chasing cattle would run out of their boot and step into the mud with their sock.

We carried sticks made out of stiff plastic piping, the kind to strike cattle with and not hurt them. We closed in on the big dry cow. She turned and faced me with bulging eyes. I yelled and swung the stick and shouted at her not to do it. Instead, she put her head down and pushed past me. The plastic echoed off her skull as she went by.

The feeder wagon's metal frame was painted red and held a glare from the low sun. It had a long rack that kept enough hay for two days. Inside were a few half-eaten bales and a piece of twine that got overlooked. It was surrounded by the shapes of hooves.

A cow that got past someone is harder to get. We walked behind the group again and tried to close in on her and move side to side as she darted. We rushed her so she couldn't turn around or have time to think, pushing her to keep trotting towards the barn. She was quick, however, and bullheaded. My father and grandfather yelled at me—*Hit her, hit her*—when she headed my way, but she lunged through us, her brisket bouncing off her chest. My father threw his stick at her after she passed. It glanced off her side. She flinched and kicked her rear legs in the air.

The sun was lowering, putting the tops of trees into silhouette. Our faces were red. It takes a while to hook and unhook the tractor from the trailer, and to try to catch her the next evening would be a failure made worse by the cost of time already spent. We headed towards the back of the lot and tried again.

We got the cow past the feeder wagon, the length of which narrowed the ground we had to cover. We converged on her, shouting and flashing our sticks. She had started to pant, a pale mist rolling from her nostrils. We told her to be good, to make good decisions, and to not be the things we called her. There wasn't much space between my father and the edge of the wagon. It seemed that we finally had her.

Then she turned and faced my father.

The dry cow rushed at my father and struck her head into his chest. He grabbed it as he was pushed back. He took a few quick steps, trying to keep his balance. Then she thrust him into the metal corner of the feeder wagon and scraped him along it.

It was the first time that I saw my father cry. He lay in the mud, tucked into himself. I had never watched an adult in pain before. Not real pain like this. My grandfather stood over him with his hands on his hips. Occasionally, he shifted his weight from one foot to another. "You're all right, aren't you?" he said. My father couldn't answer, only sob while my grandfather stared off into the distance.

I was sent to the house to fetch the pickup. The tractor wouldn't fit all of us. I was about to run off when my grandfather told me to wait. "Don't call the ambulance or get anyone upset," he said. "Your dad is fine."

My grandfather's features faded in the dusk. Although he was standing next to me, he seemed farther away. In that moment, I thought he was heartless. My father, the toughest person I knew, was writhing on the ground, and my grandfather had turned away.

What I didn't realize then was that my grandfather had a father at one time, too. That fact shaped him. The details of their relationship were few and didn't reach me until later in life. My father said that Clair was strict, but that he liked my father, so he must have had some good feelings towards my grandfather as well. I do not know what Clair died from or how long it took, but it occurred in a hospital and my grandfather watched it. He avoided hospitals and funerals ever since.

I was too young to understand the things that haunted him, and the moment was too big. The only thing I could do was run.

I sprinted up the dug road behind the barn. My heels slid up and down the back of my boots, the skin growing hot and tender. I was out of breath by the time I got to our lawn. I couldn't drive a truck yet, so I had to go into the kitchen.

My grandmother was in the living room with my mother, which was unusual, but she must have been waiting for my grandfather. I told them that Dad was hurt. They asked if he needed an ambulance. I said I thought that he did.

My father sat at the kitchen table when the ambulance arrived. He stared blankly at the wall. His face was pale. In his eyes it was apparent that he had been crying. The ambulance crew was made up of local volunteers who knew my father, which added to his embarrassment. They were obligated to take him to the hospital for a checkup and said it couldn't hurt to have things looked over, anyway. Occasionally, they glanced at us for support. My father sat there stoically, pulled into the bleached kitchen light. He was not the jovial, bantering person the ambulance volunteers knew him to be. Instead, it would be the same confused and defiant look that would appear on my grandfather's face in the years to come.

A child knows that farming is dangerous. I was told of everyone in the area who had died from rollaway wagons, tipped-over tractors, or having clothing caught in the PTO shaft behind the tractor. Death is a vague concept, though, especially at the age I was then. However, to see someone injured was another matter. It was the first time I realized that pain was natural to farming. To be a farmer meant eventually getting hurt. In the end, some come out of it and some don't.

Eventually the ambulance crew made my father sign a waiver before they left. The sound of the truck climbing the hill in front of the kitchen table seemed to linger before fading away.

"He just got scared," my grandfather said, nodding towards me.

I wasn't sure if he meant it as a defense or an accusation. Because I didn't think that I had done anything wrong, I shot back: "Well, I knew you wouldn't do anything."

He looked me over slowly. It was the first time I had spoken to my grandfather that way.

Childish Things

For a few weeks in summer, black tadpoles lined the shores of the pond, their tails flickering every time my shadow passed over them. At the age of four, I caught them in a plastic bucket. I put the pail in the water and brought it up again, carrying around the pollywogs that got washed into it. Later I learned to fish and turned over old stumps for worms or ran along the ditch grass, catching grasshoppers to put on the end of the hook. There were largemouth and smallmouth bass, and then eventually bluegills we put in to feed them. Every time I saw a bobber disappear into the pond, I knew again that the world was a good place.

Both sides of my family were farmers and teachers. The talk was mostly about farming. We used to play volleyball, especially at organized family reunions that included relatives from farther away. There wasn't much space between the pond and the dirt road, and occasionally a child was sent to fetch a ball in the water. In later years, we played Wiffle ball instead, maybe because it didn't require setting up a net. The bases were marked with shoes and hats. Sometimes the grandparents took a few swings.

Someone from every couple grilled hot dogs or hamburgers over the old tractor rim by the side of the pavilion. The fire was started by chunking up a log, pouring diesel fuel over it, and dropping a match. For most of my childhood I didn't realize that fire could be made any other way. I had seen charcoal on commercials showing suburban families enjoying themselves in a public park. As a small boy, though, I thought that life only existed on TV.

Our Harvestore silo stood at the bottom of the hill. It was the iconic symbol of farming in the eighties and nineties. It towered over the rest of the buildings and finished the idyllic image of the family farm: red barn, green fields, blue silo. At eighty feet, it was the tallest thing I knew about. The fact that my father had to climb it was incomprehensible. For many years, he dragged a six-foot by six-foot star to the top at Christmas and lit it from a handful of extension cords duct-taped together. On winter evenings we knew where our farm was when we turned onto the hill.

Back then, we could look into the valley from our pond and see three silos across the distance: my father's, my grandfather's, and one on my great uncle's old farm. The silos were visible from miles away when the houses and barns weren't. They lined up perfectly, anchoring our family to the valley.

Harvestore silos stored silage or high-moisture ear corn and were connected to large bags at the bottom. Ours bags were in our feedroom, next to the haymow. During the day the methane gas from the fermenting grass expanded into the plastic, and then the bags contracted at night when the gas cooled. It seemed like this: If the farm had a heartbeat from the vacuum pump in the parlor, then it had its lungs in the feedroom.

Eventually farms became bigger and farmers began using bunker silos instead. Harvestores made better forage, but it was quicker to get silage from a bunk, which was just two open concrete walls. That, and the unloading mechanism at the bottom of the tower sometimes broke. Still, a Harvestore silo required the type of man who had it in him to climb it, and that meant something.

We had a tiestall barn until I was ten. It was the type of barn common for farmers with blue silos. The cows were milked in the stalls and then let out to pasture at night. Barn cats ran up and down the aisle with their tails up, slinking along the rafters or sleeping in bundles in the corner of the barn. Because each cow had to be fed individually, we knew them all, including their personalities and histories. Our farm was called Hill-View Acres. As per convention, all registered calves born there started their names with Hill-View Acres and then took part of the sire's and dam's name to make their own. Considering the prefix, a name mattered, and the cattle that bore it were the farm's banner. Even the cats had their own aliases.

There is a picture of my father in a polo shirt. I had never seen him wear one in real life, as in public he seldom wavered from a dress shirt over a T-shirt and a ball cap. He is young, probably in his early twenties, and holding the halter of a big-barreled Holstein named Hill-View Acres Sexy Suzy. At the time, many farmers still classified their best cows, having the Holstein Association come to the farm to give the cattle individual scores based on the quality of their traits. Sexy Suzy "classified excellent" three times—a rare feat. The picture was professionally taken, as there was a woman who went to farms to take photographs of excellent cows so they could be hung on kitchen walls. This was a big moment for my father. He apparently decided that a polo shirt was the most formal thing he could wear while working with cattle.

There weren't any other kids within walking distance, so Grandma Dennis filled the void of a best friend. She had satellite TV and let me watch Cubs games on WGN when I didn't have to work. She made chocolate chip cookies and macaroni 'n' cheese every week because they were my favorites, and if it had been a while since my last visit, she called to tell me that she had just made one of those things. She was a faithful playmate to all my phases, from Magic the Gathering cards to wanting to make a pie out of the fish I caught at the pond. She cooked all her dishes without onions because I hated them, although she got me to eat them later in life by insisting that they would make me a better lover.

At home I played with our hired hands in between the times they had to milk. Ace and Brody were identical twins, just out of high school, and near 300 pounds each. Being brothers, they didn't mind ribbing each other, even if the other wasn't having it. Once their argument escalated to where they took hunting blades out of their trucks and started swinging them. They eventually settled it. They always showed up to milk, and that was what mattered.

Sometimes I played Wiffle ball with Ace and Brody in the lawn, one person pitching and the other behind the batter to catch. Other times we played basketball in the shop. At one point the shop housed the shredded newspaper used for bedding. It narrowed the space where we could dribble, and first we had to sweep the loose paper away. The rafters were low, so every shot had to be flat. A stray ball often bounced between all the clutter like old barn fans or plow parts on one side of the shop, or off the wall of newspaper on the other. The twins always boxed me out and made it tough to get a rebound. Afterwards they went to milk, sweat pouring down their faces.

As a last resort I played with my sister, who was three years younger than me. We turned over rocks in the creek, looking for crayfish to put into our bucket, or chased each other around the walnut tree in the lawn. We wandered around the farm, getting on tractors and pretending to drive. I told her that I could climb the silo, but she said that I couldn't and dared me to. I stood at the base and looked up at all the steps it took to reach the top. I pointed out that the ladder started too high from the ground and I couldn't reach it, or obviously I would climb it. We walked through the tiestall barn, and I'd pick out my favorite cows. I made sure she knew that they couldn't be her favorite cows, too.

Often during my childhood, I went to bed with cow shit in my hair. It didn't bother me, because the next day I woke up early and got more manure on me. "That's money," Grandpa Dennis would call it, every time someone got splattered on their skin. Whether that made sense or not, we did have money back then. We had enough grain for the cattle, and all the equipment worked. Bill collectors were rare in our driveway. Instead of sending lawyers, every Christmas the feed companies mailed calendars with naked women on them.

At some point, after eating, everyone at the pond would be sitting in a plastic chair and holding a Miller High Life or cup of iced tea. The conversation might swing around a few times to old topics, but when there was a lull, someone, maybe my father, might lift himself up and take a walk around the pond. Nearly every time he stopped at the far bank and looked down the valley, at the lives we had there. His hair was still full on top and he'd likely be wearing a Buffalo Bills shirt. Probably, since it was the nineties, he had jean shorts on. His legs were pale because he always wore pants while working. He could have been thinking about any number of things, looking over the silos.

Up to that point, my father had done nothing but farm his entire life, and that would remain true for many years. However, the most unlikely thing about my father was how much more he was than just a farmer. He had a social intelligence that was rare. It wasn't required for the type of work he did, but it drew people to him. Those who knew my father liked him. He also had a gift for finding humor in the mundane parts of life, and so even though most of what he did was to milk cows, feed them, and do fieldwork, he always had a story to tell.

Because my father had the type of face that made people comfortable around him, they told him their stories. The hoof trimmer, middle-aged and recently divorced, explained how his date grabbed his penis at a movie theater. It was too much for the hoof trimmer, so he went home soon after but returned to the theater the next night to finish the movie alone. One hired hand detailed how he had sex with his wife and immediately afterwards felt compelled to explain that while he loved her, he also loved his new girlfriend. I was in the living room once when a horse trainer broke down in front of my father, saying that he had fallen in love with an underage blind girl. At this point in his life, all the drama around my father belonged to other people.

I don't know what my father thought of his life back then. I don't know if it was harder or easier than others, or if he considered it to be one way or another. Any challenges he had would have been ordinary to either being a person in the world or a farmer in our valley, and they would have felt natural and expected. Whatever they were, he wouldn't have complained.

Eventually my father would have stood at the bank of the pond long enough to be conscious that other people might be watching him. He would then take his hands out of his pockets and walk back to his chair, fading into the sepia glare of the sun.

Internalized

THE COLDNESS HAD RECENTLY MOVED in that winter day. A few flurries fell half-heartedly from a gray sky. The mud around the barn was stiffening but still gave way under our boots. Without the sun or the comfort of snow on the banks and the tops of trees, it was a day stripped down to only what we had to do in it. I was ten and I had to feed the barn cats.

Some of the cats were drop-offs. People in town no longer wanted them or found them left over from tenants and didn't have the grit to kill them. They drove by our farm at night and threw the housecats into a nearby hedgerow. Sometimes they were eaten by coyotes before they found their way to our barn. The cats piled on top of each other in the corners of the tiestalls to keep themselves warm on cold nights. They spent nights wary of foxes and opossums, and sometimes were stepped on by cows. Some were friendly and some weren't. Regardless, the milk they got was poor recompense for the world they faced.

I reached into the bag of milk replacer—we called it calf nip—until I found the plastic cup inside. It matched the others in the kitchen cupboard because that was where they ended up. The powder smelled like cake mix but tasted much plainer. I eyed and adjusted the calf nip in the cup until it was an inch from the bottom. Then I stirred it in a bucket of warm water and poured it into the frying pan without a handle. I didn't need to call to the cats because the sight of me lifted them from the chaff and brought them scurrying to my feet.

Afterwards I went to find my father. I listened to what machinery was being used to figure out where he was. If nothing was running, then maybe I could hear him singing.

I found him in the shop. He had a broken roller chain on a vise, tapping out the pin of the ruined link with a chisel. It probably belonged to the manure spreader. The work bench next to him was covered in tools and parts lying haphazardly over each other. At the very bottom, over the wood, was decades of dust that had turned dark and muckish. It half-buried old nails, washers, and nuts of various sizes. On the floor were old toolboxes and five-gallon buckets filled with partial sets of wrenches and sockets. Things like reciprocating saws, grease gun cartridges, and pipe clamps littered the floor around him. Whatever my father needed in the shop he found quickly, which was an improbability I witnessed over and over.

I busied myself by walking through mud puddles in the driveway, breaking the thin layer of ice with the front of my boots.

"Ready for lunch?" my father asked.

Because his jeans had iodine stains in them, I knew he had not gone to the house after the morning milking. In the dusk-like shadows of the shop he had reconnected the chain to make it circular again and hung it on a nail sticking out of the wall. He started towards the house and then stopped suddenly.

"We better put the skid steer away first."

I followed him across the driveway, sometimes having to lunge forward to keep up with him. The dried goldenrod on the bank scratched against itself whenever there was a breeze. It was the time of year that a crow could call out and we would notice it and maybe follow it across the empty sky. Old tires lay against the side of the barn, their rubber cracking. The trees around us were bare and spindly. We could see, by looking beyond our farm, the orange coats of a handful of hunters spread across the valley.

The skid steer sat in front of the barn at an angle, two equidistant tracks leading to its wheels. Before feeding the cows, my father had to drive it out of the barn to make room to bring the tractor in. It was good practice to keep it under cover and only took a moment to put it back in the alley. I rocked on my heels to keep my toes warm and rubbed my mittens over my nose. In the house I was going to stand in front of the woodstove for a few minutes once I took my coat off.

My father turned the key of the skid steer. A screech echoed inside, and then a thump.

My father shut off the machine but sat there for a moment. Then he raised the safety bar and climbed out. He pushed on the latch on the back of the skid steer, leaning his weight on it to get it to give, and then swung back the metal housing.

Small, disjoined organs protruded across the length of the radiator. The tissue was pink, nearly bright, and folded in on itself. Because the engine had only been on for a moment, it was clear that the thin wisps of steam were animal in origin. A matted fringe outlined a parcel of flesh, and from that I could tell what cat it had been.

My father picked up a long tendril of intestine and held it between two fingers. He stared at it, as if he, too, were surprised that a few seconds ago that had been a cat we saw slinking through the barn or sidling up to the milk dish.

I looked at my father wide-eyed with a fleeting emptiness, waiting for his guidance on how to react. He knew that he had to be a father in that moment, and he didn't have long to decide how.

My grandfather, as I imagine it, would have shrugged and said, "That's life." And he would be right, either in the way that our lifestyle was not short on uncomfortable sights or that the lives of barn cats often ended in mutilation, whether by being run over or jumping through wall fans. Or, a generation ago, my grandfather might have told my father to buck up if he started to cry. Those would have been the examples my father would have had at hand. That's how most farmers' sons his age were taught.

Instead, my father threw the intestine at me.

It landed on the front of my coat and stuck there.

The piece of bowel stretched lengthwise across my zipper, the top of it hanging over my collar. I pulled my head back, both to try to look at it and to keep it from touching my skin. It was musty, and closer to the smell of earth than I expected. I peeled it off me and held it in my hand, the end of the tissue twisting gently.

Years later, that day would be flooded with retrospection. My father knew, as most fathers would, that it was up to him to shape the moment. Instead of looking to shield my innocence or lessen my hurt, or even callous me against the world ahead, some instinct told him that there was a more important message I needed to know: that sometimes farming is absurd. It can be un-clinical and illogical, and to most people it wouldn't make sense. And, despite all that, we have to keep doing it.

I threw the intestine back at him. He ducked and the string of entrails fell over a tractor rut behind him. Then he scraped up a handful of pulp from the radiator grooves and flung it at me. Viscera fell over my shoulders and knit hat.

We threw the dismembered cat at each other until we went in for lunch.

Going Big

ONE HUNDRED CLEAN HOLSTEINS spread across the sidehill. When they were let out to pasture in the morning, they followed the dirt paths worn into the ground by generations of cattle at Hill-View Acres. They heaved single file, their broad heads bobbing, until they reached taller grass and diverged. They advanced slowly, nearly equidistant, toward the far end of the pasture. In the summer afternoon the hillside flickered as their tails slapped at flies. Below them, cars began to pull up to the barn.

I stood outside the newly built milking parlor. The brass knob of the door shone, inviting someone to open it and look in. The concrete around it was swept clean. Someone had taken a broom and knocked away all the cobwebs from the preexisting walls in front of it. Being ten, I hadn't been allowed around the barn alone while the construction was going on, so I was still getting used to the new shape of the farm.

My father set down two workhorses next to me and mumbled to himself that he could probably find two more. Then he came back and put plywood over them.

The parlor was built into the middle of the old tiestall barn where my father had milked cows from the age of seventeen. The front half of the old barn remained as it was, with block-glass windows and stalls still in place. Behind the parlor, however, was an expanse of grooved concrete that was the holding area for cows waiting to be milked. That was connected to the recently finished freestall barn. Where I stood, outside the parlor, was where the new barn forced its way into the old barn. It was the threshold of a passageway, and it was supposed to lead to good things.

A woman I didn't know appeared next to me. She pressed on the plywood held up by the workhorses, thought for a moment, and then leaned more of her weight on it.

"It'll do," she said.

She began carrying bain-maries through the milk house door and lining them up on the board. Faint steam lifted around the handles. The smell of food in a barn would have been contradictory if we weren't already accustomed to the odors of cattle. After she had brought out three or four double boilers, she came back with Kaiser rolls and plastic cutlery. She lifted the lids off the beef, the beans, and the potato salad to check them one more time. Then she turned to me. "Looks good, doesn't it?"

My mother passed by and told me not to eat anything yet.

Next, several younger men carried folding tables through the barn. They were in their late twenties to early thirties, each wearing clean brown shoes and a padded vest with their company's logo on it. They set up near the wall, unfurling standing banners and organizing the hats and pens they brought to give away. They greeted each other in a manner that revealed their familiarity. One came from M&T Bank, while others were from an agricultural supply firm or the multinational that had built the parlor. They all represented institutions that made money from our expansion regardless of what was going to happen to us.

Once he was set up, one of the bank representatives came over to me and crouched. "Big day, isn't it?"

A cat brushed along my pant legs. I picked it up and stroked it as a way to show that I was the one who belonged here.

"Is that a nice cat?" the employee asked.

"It's a nice one," I said.

The first farmers stepped out of the daylight at the front of the barn, looking around until they spotted us. They slowly walked over with their hands in their pockets.

My father explained it like this: My parents had not talked about enlarging their operation before they went to the yearly meeting with their bank, but they were aware that other farms had done it. There was a growing fever in the industry to leave behind the labor-intensive tiestall barns that limited cow numbers and build bigger freestall barns with parlors that allowed more cows to be milked at once. It was later implied that, in the same way farmers became a little envious of those who expanded, so did financial institutions who had heard of other lenders signing the papers to those farmers. This was the atmosphere of March 1994 when, as my father told it, the manager of M&T Bank in Prattsburg, New York, leaned over the desk and said, "So, you're making money. Do you want to make some more?"

Even though it might have felt like it, that moment didn't arrive without a context. Many years before, in 1977, author Wendell Berry debated Nixon's secretary of agriculture, Earl Butz, at Manchester College in Indiana. Berry advocated for better farming over bigger agriculture, suggesting that smaller farms created cultural and social capital within a community. In contrast, Butz declared: "Adapt or die." The seventies were good for crop farmers and they heeded Butz's call to expand, only to charge headfirst into the farm crisis of the eighties. By the end of the decade, one-third of the farms held two-thirds of the nation's debt. The number of suicides marked the consequences of following Butz's advice.

As a child in the nineties growing up in New York State, I had the vague notion that there had been a farm crisis, but never got the sense that it bothered the adults any more than me. In addition to agriculture having a short memory, farming sectors are diverse and don't all rise and fall on the same tide. High grain prices are typically bad for dairy farmers in that they raise the price of feeding cattle and the costs of planting. Coincidentally, the farmgate price for milk—the payment farmers themselves received—was relatively high in the early eighties. The pain of the "farm crisis," as far as my father and the neighbors remembered it, was never registered in the dairy industry. Neither were, it turned out, the lessons to be learned from it.

The American dairy industry began to feel different in the nineties. Prices had started to become more volatile, and an oversupply of milk was hurting the sector. The farmgate price in the early nineties was lower than that of the early eighties, while costs had risen. For the first time in decades, dairy farmers were starting to get nervous. Maybe not everyone realized it back then, but the industry was at a crossroads.

My mother described the decision differently. She said that my father never wanted to expand, but my grandfather talked him into it. My grandfather insisted that to get bigger was the only way to keep farming. By then, such advice was conventional. My grandfather had been milking in a 150-cow freestall barn for thirty years.

"But we're happy in the tiestall barn," my mother said.

"We won't be able to pay the electricity bill," my father said.

She thought he got that line from my grandfather.

The construction company broke ground on the new 200-cow freestall barn in May 1994, erecting it next to the 100-cow tiestall barn. That summer my father milked fifty cows in the old barn and then put them outside to bring in the other fifty. Even if my father could be excited about it, he was too busy moving cattle around to take in the moment. The freestall operation with bunker silos was going to be more efficient, nonetheless, so the awkwardness of the transition was a small price to pay.

The barn was finished in autumn. The building still smelled like the timber poles that held it up and the grooved concrete was pristine, not yet splattered with manure. I snuck over the gates to dribble my basketball through it, racing up and down the empty stalls and pretending I was Michael Jordan. The parlor looked like an achievement of technology, with milkers lined on both sides and connected to the main flow channel. A pump sat regally in the corner, ready to drive the system.

The metal cattle dividers and back pans were crisp and bright, the walls white, and the windows above let in clean light. It all added up to a feeling of moving forward.

Before any cow could step into the new barn, however, we had to wait for the open house.

M&T asked my parents if they wanted to celebrate their new farming venture. The bank would organize it themselves and even provide the catering. My mother said yes before my father could answer. She spent all her days in the barn or raising children, and welcomed any social event she could get. My father folded his arms and said nothing.

M&T gave my parents a large plywood cutout of a cow eating roses with a teddy bear on its back. It didn't fit the style that I associate with my mother, but since it was her only decoration, she leaned it against the young maple tree in the lawn. Pickups parked along the edge of the driveway and around the milk house, and when there was no more room, pulled onto the grass before falling silent and rocking to a halt. Visitors filtered towards the barn in long, slow strides, nodding at others doing the same.

In the same way that the freestall barn was fresh and unsullied before having its first cow milked in it, the remaining half of the tiestall barn was also groomed, as it was about to take its last one. All the manure was cleared out as much as possible, the walls were whitewashed, and the floor was heavily dusted with lime. It radiated whiteness, even if it was not the bride that day. However, visitors simply passed through it on their way to see the new construction.

I had only seen other farmers at shows and the yearly cattle sale. I walked among them now, somewhat awestruck to have them all there, in our own barn. Even at that age I had the sense that a barn was a personal space where repetitions played out every day with little change. To see others standing there, too, even though our new routine was still ahead of us, made it feel like a life event. They greeted each other by saying, "How are they milking?" and then crossed their arms and mused on how foolish the act of farming was. It was an old communion that I was privileged to witness.

My parents stood near the food while others took turns gathering around them with Styrofoam plates in their hands. My mother smiled and laughed and received well-wishes by emphatically dipping her head, while my father muttered, "Thanks." Once in a while, he had to explain how long the barn took to build and if they would start milking in it that week. He was biding his time until the construction company took the group on a tour of the new additions. Every so often one of the representatives came up to him to shake his hand and congratulate him loudly in front of the other farmers. It was meant to spark enough jealousy to make someone else take the plunge and expand. It worked, because farms were doing it all over the country.

Before the day was over, someone had taken a picture of my parents standing behind the plywood cow. My mother had makeup on, as well as her good coat, and she was smiling brightly. My father wore a hoodie and a Bills hat. He had a playfully cunning look, like when joking with my sister and me as children, but you couldn't tell what he was really thinking. The background was filled with models of Fords and Dodges that are no longer found on the road. I didn't realize until years later that the cow's eyelids drooped and the roses it ate appeared nearly wilted, suggesting an entirely different emotion than I had taken it for back then.

The Trade-Off

THE PUCK WAS TWO CAPS FROM TEAT DIP DRUMS joined together with black electrical tape. The sticks were the stiff plastic piping we tapped on cows' thurls to head them towards the holding area. The goals were the legs of the steps on both ends of the parlor. When the last cow on either side of us had a milker on, my father and I grabbed the sticks and met in the middle of the pit. We lowered our shoulders, bent our knees, and planted our boots against the rubber mat.

"You're going down, Punk," my father said.

Then one of us dropped the puck and our sticks clashed. The noise sent a shiver among the cows.

Like Ace and Brody, my father pushed me backwards with his weight. My boots had no grip on the mat. I tried to dig the puck out from between his legs. When I was at a loss, I hit his stick frantically and kicked it if I had to. The few small windows in the parlor showed the morning darkness, but the fluorescent bulbs above us filled the pit with bleached light. I grabbed the pipeline along the wall for leverage as he inched me backwards. When I leaned against my father, I could smell the manure and iodine in his clothes. Sometimes he stepped aside and let me fall forward.

The cows pinned their ears back as they watched us. The new barn had been a difficult adjustment for them. Many of the old herd had to be caught with a halter and dragged into the parlor. Some cows took to the freestalls and some did not, instead lying in the manure in the alley. Those that refused to use the stalls had to be culled. Fresh concrete is abrasive and hard on cattle, and some got banged up. In the tiestalls, the cows had names, ones that started with Hill-View Acres, but now they

45

only had numbers. Earl Butz's law of economics was just as real to them as to the farmers: If they couldn't adapt, they were sent on a truck for beef. It was the price of being a number.

To fill out capacity quickly, my parents bought another herd from a farmer a few hours away. They were freestall cows, which made them unremarkable, but they didn't have to be trained. They went into the parlor, used the stalls, and tried to find their place among the other cows. At the auction an old man told my father not to buy anything there, because that farmer had problems with high somatic cell counts. The old man was telling the truth, as it later turned out that many of them had mastitis and other infections.

The freestall system, naturally, did have advantages. Milking more cattle allowed my father to hire more help. Using bunkers was a quicker and less dangerous way to feed cattle than to have to wait for the silage to unload from a Harvestore silo. The three-month slurry storage behind the freestalls permitted my father to spread manure when it suited him better, as opposed to spreading it daily in the tiestall barn.

Too young to help, I mostly watched the trucks back up to the barn to deliver the new cattle. Still, I felt the change too. Every morning, we had drawn a pitcher of milk from our bulk tank and drank it like water. During the day, the cream shifted towards the top of the container and left rings on the plastic after each cup we poured. However, as my mother explained, we had brought cows into the herd that we didn't know. While our original cows didn't have Johne's, a condition that leads to Crohn's disease in humans, we couldn't be sure of the new cows. Our milk pitcher got stacked in the back of the cupboard. The fact that a farmer could be divested from the thing he made was an uneasy omen.

The friction of the duct tape over the wet rubber made the puck drone when we hit it. I yelled *Hey!* when my father kicked it ahead of him. When I shot and made it, I danced. If it went wide, I had to contort my body to reach it from behind the pump, or lay on my stomach on the top step and fish it from the back wall with the end of my stick. Then we started again in the middle, counting down and dropping the teat dip caps.

Sixteen Holsteins surrounded us as we played parlor hockey. Milk flowed through the plastic windows below their teats and slowly thinned away like an hourglass. If one of us got checked into the wall below it or if our elbow grazed its hock, then that cow stopped chewing and shifted on its rear legs. Inevitably, before long, one of the cows kicked the milker off.

The score didn't get very high before we had to change the cows in the parlor and reset the game.

Parlor hockey was short-lived. Although I enjoyed it, because I was now milking and driving a tractor, part of me thought that it didn't fit with becoming older. In fact, it surprised me that my father came up with the idea. A lot of time was invested in making the new system of farming work. Now, more than ever, it had to be treated like a business. The tiestall cows were already struggling in the freestall barn, and our shouts didn't encourage them to let their milk down. Parlor hockey wasn't a good farming practice.

Looking back, I think my father missed something human about the act of farming. To whatever extent he was forced into the freestall barn, it now shaped his days—as it would for many other farmers who kept milking. The parlor was where he started every morning from there on out, and he had to make peace with that. He had to bring who he thought he was through its door.

Still, there was more to it than that. He had to be a father and a farmer at the same time. It would have been easy to let one reduce the other. Instead, he made sure to spend time with me while I was still young. We played games and talked about school and sports in between putting the milkers on, and we did our best to pretend those days didn't feel like a childhood ending. I don't think he was given that growing up.

Maybe he wanted to show me, while I was a boy, that I would always come before the farm. In the relationship between fathers and sons, they have to figure out what is going to hold them together. For those like us, it was always going to be farming. How that farm stood between us, however, had to be decided.

After milking, my father swept the bunks. They lined both sides of the freestall barn's center aisle. When the cows put their necks forward to eat, some of the silage got nudged out of reach. My father took the pitchfork off the nail it was hanging on and started at the near end of the barn. He moved along the tiles of the bunks mechanically, swinging the fork back and then into the silage, thrusting forward a pile bigger than its width. Streaks of forage were left behind where it overflowed the fork. Sometimes he had to put a work shoe on the tines and lean his weight on them, but he never lost the cadence with which he moved. When he finished one side of the alleyway, he started down the other.

In the tiestall barn, my father fed each cow individually, pushing a grain cart and breaking a square bale in the alley to spread. Each cow's diet was individual according to their lactation. In the freestall barn, his herd was split into two groups. He backed up the mixer wagon on the side of the barn that housed the higher producers to give them extra silage. Sweeping the bunks was a brief but physical act that might have reminded my father of the tiestall barn. It was pleasantly inefficient and made him feel that he was serving his cattle like he used to.

On seeing him, cows began to lift themselves and amble towards the bunks. Like my father, they, too, started to figure out the new routine. They had manure on their legs and their coats looked rougher. A few of them limped as they backed out of the stalls. My father tried not to think about it.

Sexy Suzy's tall withers and wide barrel made her stick out from the rest of the herd. Implicit in having a three-time excellent cow is the suggestion that the owner knows cattle and how to breed them. Maybe, too, that the person is a good farmer. Suzy's angular body and color patterns made her look like the plastic true-type model made by the Holstein Association. There were pictures of my mother, my sister, and me on the kitchen wall, but the only time my father was inside a frame, he was holding Sexy Suzy. She was the pennant of the Hill-View Acres prefix and evidence to the world that my father had taken the farm given to him and done right by it.

The mixer wagon sat in the alleyway of the barn, between the two groups of cattle. Although the John Deere it was attached to was older, my father had bought other, larger equipment. This included a Ford 8870, two big slurry tanks, two silage wagons, and a bigger plow. My father knew better than to internalize the congratulations of dealers who shook his hand when he passed them a check. He appreciated the newness of those machines and whatever comfort or convenience they had over the old equipment, but he didn't give into thinking it was progress.

At least that is how I reconstruct those early days in the freestall barn for my father. I was too young at the time to be told what thoughts he had or to try to read them in his actions. My assumptions are in hindsight and based on how I knew my father to be. In that way, I also think that he realized that it did no good to hold onto reservations anymore. The barn was built, and the bank held his new mortgage. He was on the vanguard of new farming methods. Farming has always changed as technology advanced. On some level, it was exciting. He lost nothing from admitting that.

My father continued the steady step-thrust, step-thrust work with the fork. Sometimes, playfully, he tossed the silage into the face of a cow to see her shake her head. Pigeons shifted in the rafters above him, bunched together under the ceiling. They had already made nests in the joints. It wasn't cold, so the rolltop doors were open on both ends, allowing a small breeze through the alleyway. He felt it in the dampness around his collar. He looked out of the barn while he swept the bunks, into the glare of daylight, his mind wandering.

When my father was done, he hung the pitchfork back on the nail. He didn't get into the tractor right away but remained in the aisle with his hands on his hips, looking over the cattle again.

Sexy Suzy stood in front of the stalls, staring back.

Still looking at him, she fell to her knees, and then to her side, her big chest rocking. Air rushed through her nostrils as she exhaled.

My father froze. His own breath had stopped. Finally, he ducked under the brisket bar and ran up to her. "Come on," he said, kneeing her in the ribs. "Come on. Get up."

He slapped her chest with an open palm. It echoed dully. "Come on, now," he said. Some of the cattle circled around him, chewing their cuds. Others still lingered around the bunks.

My father shook Suzy's neck chain and then poked her in the thigh. He pressed her ribs again, where her heart would be, and simulated a pumping motion. He stood up and looked around. Sunlight reflected off the clean aluminum of the high ceiling. The timber poles had drip patterns from a preservative. The metal stalls shone. My father turned and kicked Suzy in the face over and over again, his boot striking her in the muzzle.

The cow's head rolled to the side, her eyes staring into the future.

Notes on the American Dairy Industry

In some ways, the idea of America doomed its family farms.

While dairy farming always had its ups and downs and farm sizes have increased since the founding of the Republic, the math started to change in the nineties. Old-timers swore that milk swung in seven-year cycles, but this felt different, evidence that the industry was getting tougher.

Overproduction was also not a new problem. Ever since World War II, the United States marveled at its own ability to make farm products, sometimes even suggesting that it was America's duty to "feed the world." However, none of the milk that farmers made saved starving families across the planet; instead it all stayed in the United States and lowered the prices farmers received. Previously, when the price of milk dropped too low, the US government bought excess volume off the market and stored it as nonfat dry milk, reducing supply and boosting the farmer's milk check. This type of intervention, however, was seen as inefficient, and eventually the political patience for it ran out.

When it came down to it, the US government had two choices. The first was to work towards supply control through a quota system. Farmers would only be paid full price for the amount of milk they had a quota to produce, and the national supply would be mostly based on how much Americans consumed themselves. Canada, Iceland, and, at the time, the European Union had milk quotas in place. It was not a perfect system, as farmers entering the industry had to purchase the right to a quota, and it meant not being able to take advantage of international markets during times they were lucrative. However, it did lead to a stable system with higher milk prices. In countries still with a quota, herds of thirty to fifty cows continue to support entire families.

However, the United States was just coming out of the Cold War. Americans were in the frame of mind to idealize the free market, considering it an emblem of national identity. It was often conflated with personal freedom, and politically, when it came to agricultural policy, it was an easy sell.

Nonetheless, an unregulated market simply doesn't work in dairy farming, and it's easy to see why. Farmers have little negotiating power with large manufacturers and multinational retailers, and as became evident later, the cooperative that most of them were forced into did more harm than good. More importantly, milk is both a flow product and perishable. Farmers can't store their milk until the price gets higher, and they can't turn the cows off when the price is too low. Milk leaves their farm regardless of the price they'll get for it. All this makes agricultural markets too complex to leave unregulated. However, in the shadow of the Cold War, everyone knew how to defeat an idea: call it "communist." Economists who favored supply control were told to go back to Gorbachev.

Instead, the American dairy industry became a free-for-all. The response to lower prices from overproduction was to encourage farmers to produce more. To compensate for tighter margins, they had to get more cows. It was no coincidence that, at the same time, agribusiness was on the rise. Regardless of the milk check, whenever a farm milked more cows, the agricultural corporations around it made more money. These firms were the biggest sponsors and advertisers of the magazines farmers read. In the end, these publications all told the farmer the same thing: if you're not moving forward, you're going backwards. Butz's reanimated figure hovered over the dairy industry.

The 1996 Farm Bill, also called the Federal Agricultural Improvement and Reform (FAIR) Act, was a major shift in US agricultural policy. Although previous farm bills had started to move away from supply management, the FAIR Act sought to kill it entirely in the United States, both in practice and as a concept. The biggest proponents of the act were crop farmers, who did not want to limit how much land they could plant. It was not inconsequential that crop prices were high in 1996.

In regard to the dairy industry, the FAIR Act removed the price support applied to milk. Dairy farmers had been guaranteed a base price, achieved by the government purchasing milk when volume exceeded demand and storing it as butter or powder. Once the supply of milk was no longer regulated, the milk price became more volatile and typically low. To phase out the milk price support, dairy farmers were to receive decreasing payments from 1997 to 2000. The purpose of the 1996 Farm Bill was to increase the "market orientation" of agricultural sectors in the United States, although low prices forced politicians to reinstate milk price supports. Even if the bill eventually failed to end all milk subsidies, it did establish the policy ideology that the United States would follow and paved the way to increasingly reduce the support given to smaller dairy farms in the future.

In short, it was now every farmer for themselves.

II.
The World Beyond

When the Cowboys Came Around

I SAT ON A DUSTY CUSHION, tucked between the door and my father's work shoe. My knees were pulled to my chest, and sometimes I had to shift again to get comfortable. Beneath me, the cut hay was narrowed into windrows to be later chopped into silage. It was peculiar to be folded so small and see a field pass by backwards. Everything one does in their early teens is to make themselves appear bigger and fuller, but to ride in the haybine, I had to sit on the floor. A grease gun, wrenches, and old cassette tapes were on either side of me. Emily crouched in the other corner. She stared past her reflection to the wheel turning below her and barked every time the haybine changed speed.

Earlier that day my grandfather's truck pulled into our driveway. He had already passed by the house once, so we knew he had driven along our property to look at the fields. My father walked across the lawn to meet him and asked if he wanted a cup of coffee.

"We should just start chopping ourselves, shouldn't we?" my grandfather said.

My father tried to hide half a smile. "Our turn will come."

My grandfather stood with his hands on his hips and looked up the hill, from the hay to the sky and back to the fields again. Then he got in his truck and went home.

My father and I glanced at each other. My father betrayed that this wasn't a usual summer week only by being less talkative. Usually, my grandfather would have shown even less signs of being anxious, his calm reserve being a defining feature. Frustration over something he couldn't change didn't fit. Even if everyone has bad days.

The haybine slowed as my father turned it on the headlands. When

Emily barked he would yell her name, but she couldn't be reasoned with any more than the inanimate tools beneath her. She was addicted to riding in trucks or machinery and would starve herself to death in the haybine if it never stopped running. My father stared over me to the grass in front of him, seldom blinking. The throttle had the shape of his hand worn over the metal. With his thumb he lifted the head of the haybine whenever he saw a stone or woodchuck hole, or pulled back to stop the machine if a fawn was crouching in the hay below.

My father was particularly gentle with the haybine. Usually he drove slowly, scanning the grass for anything that could break a blade. The machine crawled along while it played Fleetwood Mac's *Rumours*, and if not that, Cher's *Heart of Stone*. Often my father sang along. He might tap the steering column for a drumbeat. This time, though, he didn't. Instead, he occasionally glanced up at the empty roads by the field.

Sometimes I looked over my shoulder to watch the theater of hay below me. The tops of timothy or rye swayed in the breeze, if there was one, before bending below the cutter bar. Chaff circled in front of the glass and settled on the vibrating metal of the haybine's head. Sometimes the stalks parted in a wiry streak as an unseen rabbit darted out of the way.

Finally, a dump truck descended the hill. It slowed as it passed hayfields to see what had been cut and then pulled into the field that my father was working in. The driver parked on the headlands and then leaned on the hood, also watching the hill. His shirt was stained and his collar was stretched from being scratched at on hot days. Eventually another truck came and then an old tractor with a diverter on the back. They eased to a stop over a windrow and let their machines idle. Sinking back into their seats, they reached through the open window and drummed the outside of their doors with rough fingers. At this point in the summer, they had nothing to say to each other. Finally, the chopper crested the knoll, lumbering over the pavement in road gear.

"Well," my father said, pushing open the door so I could descend the steps. "Showtime."

I climbed into the Gator and drove around the large parade of equipment suddenly at the end of our field. I nodded to the people standing there with their arms folded or kicking at the tires of whatever they drove. They stared at me for a while and then nodded, too. Although I know that's not how it happened, I imagine that they all came down our hill at once in a cloud of dust, not unlike how posses rode into small Western towns in the movies. In total, the custom choppers were the closest thing we had to cowboys in western New York.

The chopper itself was worth three times our house and seemed about as large. It made us feel primitive as it passed by. After the head man talked to my father, everyone climbed into their cabs and turned on their machines. The headlands grew hazy in the swell of exhaust. It wasn't cheap to hire the custom choppers, but it allowed us to fill a bunk in days instead of months. The expense was a calculated risk: getting all the hay cut early and the trench packed quickly made for better silage and therefore more milk.

When the custom choppers arrived, we had to be ready because they hit the fields in a flurry. My father, like most farmers, cut his own hay to reduce costs. He needed to knock enough fodder down before the choppers came and then to stay ahead of them. On these days, my father kept a sandwich behind the seat and barely stopped to piss. The head of the haybine rocked up and down as he raced the lengths of our grass.

When we were on our own, we entered the fields in patient, eight-load days. My grandfather chopped, I packed, and my father brought the empty wagon onto the headlands and took the full wagon back to the trench. The speed with which the custom outfit removed the forage from our land was jarring. They diverted three windrows into one and ran their chopper over it, spitting the silage into the dump trucks driving next to it. The trucks rotated in and out by the chopper, rushing back to our trench to dump the load in the pit. There, I spread the silage and ran over it repeatedly to pack it down and press out the oxygen, allowing it to ferment.

When I was younger, we hired Tom Perkins to pack the trench. He had one of those local family names that required sorting through which ones were good and which ones weren't, but he always showed up and worked, and that was all one could ask.

I would finish heifer chores and bring the loader tractor to the trench. Sometimes Tom was already there, leaning against the pole of the grain shed and smoking a cigarette. "Women are evil," he told me, blowing out smoke. "They'll rip your heart out."

Tom was going through a bad divorce and, the best that I could tell, was not taking it in stride. I was twelve or thirteen and years away from being kissed. I didn't have much to offer back, other than to nod quietly.

"You can't trust them," he said, flicking his cigarette into the weeds and climbing into the tractor. "They're all bitches."

It was a hard summer for the crew of the custom outfit. It's one thing for someone to spend all day in their own fields, where the shape of the ground has already left its imprint inside them. These men, however, went from farm to farm, passing over someone else's land for a week or two at a time, and then moved on. One thing about Westerns is how little the characters seem to need and how easily they accept their fates. The men hired to make up the crew were those who weren't working but who could work, and in an economically depressed area such as Allegany County, that type of man was easily found. They ran the fields until dark each day of the week, only getting a day off when it rained. Sometimes, after a day of hauling silage, one or two of them lingered around the trench in the dusk. My father would hand them a Miller High Life and make small talk while they turned to silhouettes.

As I got older, fourteen or fifteen, I packed the trench myself when the custom choppers arrived.

The trucks came fast, dumping their loads at the base of the pile. There wasn't much time to spread the wet silage over the mound and press it in with the tractor tires. The choppers cost us hundreds of dollars per hour. I didn't want to slow them down.

I thrust the corner of the bucket into the dumped load. The tractor hesitated, dropping to a low drawl when it met the resistance of the silage, until the silage gave way in front of it. I angled away the load, slowly raising the bucket to apply the silage evenly. The silage already in the pit had started to brown, but a new load left by a dump truck was dark green and shimmered with moisture. I sat at the edge of the tractor seat, peering through the windshield. My body tipped forward when I drove ahead and rocked back when I reversed. The smell of warm silage rose up around me and came in through the open windows. The air in the cab was heavy and suspended me in it.

Some drivers waved when they brought the first load and some did not. Mostly they looked ahead without expression. Before long I began to understand the trucks' rhythm, sensing them backing up to the pit before I saw them. The trucks came faster if the chopper moved to a field closer to the trench. There was no chance to daydream or wonder about anything but the forage in front of me. The radio hit a dead spot and then reappeared as I rose up and down the pile, but my mind filled in the missing lyrics without realizing it. My hand rested on the gearstick, my fingers shaped around it. My shoulders ached from turning around the same way to watch the tires. When I pushed the gas to get up the pile or move the silage, I felt like I was giving more of myself, too. Most days Emily rode with me and she barked every time we changed direction, bookending the tractor's movements and taking its place in the other rhythms of packing the trench.

I saw myself as bookish and unnatural around engines. I couldn't fix machinery by myself, and I wasn't useful with my hands in the shop. This made me wonder if I had it in me to be a farmer myself. While packing the trench, however, I didn't have the chance to think of myself in any other way. For a day at a time, my world was small and rectangular and frantic, down to spreading silage out and running over it before more silage came. Sometimes in my haste my work shoe slipped off the clutch and the tractor jerked. It made Emily jump at the wheels. Gray dust and small debris fell into the silage when I accidentally scraped the side wall and left a divot in the concrete. It joined other marks there as my part in a collective history.

There was a lot on the line when the custom choppers came to our farm. Something could have broken, on our equipment or theirs, that would have waylaid everything, or the weather could have made getting the silage difficult. More importantly, my father and I had to hold up our part of it. They chopped much quicker than he could mow, so he had to get up early to get the milking done and be in the field as soon as the dew dried. Once he started, he stayed there until dark. If the haybine broke a blade or grass jammed in the rollers, he had to fix it as quickly as possible. In the same way, if I slowed down the trucks at the trench, I would have frustrated the crew and cost our family money we couldn't afford. It took something from both of us to keep going like that for weeks at a time.

In the end, we were tested and we came through. The outside farming community confirmed us as a father and son on a farm. I was a teenager and embarrassed at receiving compliments, but my father said that I did good.

How farmers fed their cows is one way to follow the history of the industry. During my father's childhood, portable grinders made it possible to give more grain to cattle, resulting in more milk and faster-growing heifers. Everyone who had a dairy farm in the eighties and nineties used the blue Harvestore silos that allowed them to make and store silage. Then it was decided that trenches in the ground or with concrete sides were cheaper, were easier, and made better forage. For a little while, custom choppers were the way many farmers got their silage.

Nonetheless, like the blue silos, the days of the custom choppers were limited. They were hired by family farms, and at the turn of the century, these farms were disappearing. Those that held on could not pay for it in a struggling industry. The few large farms that remained kept getting bigger and soon had their own teams of men to make their silage. They didn't need to hire anyone else. One day, the only cowboys we ever had in western New York stopped coming back.

The Colors of Milking

I WAS ON MY WAY TO THE BARN when I stopped and shielded the sun with my palm. Since we lived in a valley, it took a while for a vehicle cresting the hill to reach our driveway. I couldn't read the lettering on the side of the white van, but it was blue, and I knew it said DeLaval. I waited by the milk house door, knowing there was no sense going into the barn and having to come out again.

Inside the van was DJ, or as we called him, the Soap Guy. He pieced together an income from several part-time trades, one of them as a representative for a multinational that sold milking supplies. We bought teat dip from him in fifteen-gallon drums, chlorine and acid for the milkers' wash system, and brown paper towels we used to wipe the udders. DJ purchased the supplies directly from DeLaval and resold them to farmers. Considering how little money farmers were making at the time and how difficult it became to get payment out of them, even my father once remarked: "That's a tough way to make a living."

A dairy farm had certain regular visitors at the barn. In addition to the Soap Guy, the milkman came every other day to empty the bulk tank, and semen salesmen arrived monthly with flyers of different bulls. Uncle Donny, Grandpa Dennis' brother, hauled cattle after he quit farming. Even into his seventies, he limped into our barn and leaned on a cane while he told us how much calves and bred heifers were bringing, and who had their corn in and who didn't. These people were how news arrived on the farm. They brought with them rumors and opinions, and to a young teenager, every once in a while something they said sounded like a proverb. "Once farming is in your blood you can never get it out," or "There are two types of people: those who can walk away from a farm and those who can't. Those who can leave should not just walk but run." Then we would smile and nod our heads and say, "Ain't that the truth."

Bill collectors also drove up to the milk house door. Dairy farming is a cash flow business: our family used each milk check to pay the most pressing invoices. Even in the best of times, it was a balancing act, leaving some bills unpaid. If left too long, someone pulled into our driveway.

My father usually met the bill collector in front of the barn, where they began an awkward but choreographed dance. My father was asked how he was doing and how the cows were milking and what about this weather. One of them brought up local news if they had it: a high school merger, a bad accident, an official caught embezzling. If they didn't, they went to national politics. They folded their arms and nodded their heads at each other. Eventually, my father mentioned when the next milk check was coming and said he would "put something in the mail." Sometimes the bill collector's shoulders suddenly relaxed, released from his obligation. As the years went on, however, my father stopped coming out of the barn. If I saw the debt collector first, my father would ask which vehicle the man drove and tell me to say that he was in the field.

I put my work shoe on the old railroad tie that enclosed the flowerbed by the milk house, but then decided that was too much like a teenager trying to look cool. Instead, I slipped my hands into my pockets, which was my default posture. I thought about going back into the milk house to come out just as DJ pulled up so I didn't have to think about how I should stand, waiting. I could have rolled out the empty blue drum from along the barn wall for him to take back, but it was already near where he parked anyway. When my sister and I were little, my mother cut one of the drums in two and fashioned Halloween costumes out of the halves. She put a hole in the middle so we could slip into them and made shoulder straps to help suspend the barrels around our waists. She turned the drums into horses and made us fake legs to look like we were riding them. We won $25 at the costume contest in the fire hall. Several years later, my father made a raft out of the teat dip drums to use in our pond.

The Soap Guy's van didn't slow down as it neared our driveway. Instead, it drove past, climbing up the hill again.

I went to find my father.

It turned out, we couldn't afford fifteen-gallon barrels of teat dip anymore. They were a small investment each time, and the kind for which we didn't have the cash flow. Instead, my mother brought home small jugs from the ag store, which we then started diluting. Eventually that got too expensive, and my father began watering down Clorox instead. We had to be careful not to make it too strong, so we didn't burn the cows' teats. We used rolls of Bounty instead of the sturdy brown dairy paper towels we got from DJ, ripping each square in half first. Even worse, in another year or two we couldn't have the fuel truck stop anymore and instead relied on however many covered buckets of diesel we could pay for at the gas station.

These changes were small, but they distorted an essential routine. Pumping the lever to fill the jug before milking was an inherent part of our work. In fact, the blue drum and brown paper towels were the colors of the morning milking and put hues to our memories of it later. When we gave up the poignant smell of teat dip, it seemed like we lost something more.

Donuts and Secondhand Cows

THE ONLY TIME MY MOTHER BOUGHT DONUTS was when there was a loan meeting. Because they came in a white box with wax paper between them, they seemed like something above our station. My sister and I had to do the regular housework, but when a loan officer visited, my mother mopped the floor and made sure that all our barn boots were neatly stacked in the mudroom.

I usually didn't know if the loans in question were with M&T Bank, from when my parents expanded the farm, or with the Farm Service Agency (FSA), which dealt out spring operating credit needed to buy seed and fertilizer before planting. Any person with a plaid shirt and a folder of papers was generalized into a bank man. It was probably awkward for these people to come into someone's kitchen and dictate the terms of a family's livelihood. This is only conjecture, but I suspect that whether they took a donut when they sat down foretold the type of news they were about to deliver.

When my sister and I were young, we were told to stay outside during loan meetings. We'd play in the creek, one of us periodically climbing the bank to see if the stranger's car was still there. By the time we were teenagers, we knew to leave the house. We never bothered asking how it went, because my parents were never forthcoming with details.

When I was older, maybe sixteen or seventeen, I asked my father if I could sit in on a loan meeting.

Taking over Grandpa Dennis' farm had been my plan since I was young. Now, I was nearly the same age my father was when he got his own farm. It would be useful to understand the business dealings of the operation. Not only was I heir to that life, but I had worked on the farm every day since my twelfth birthday. I thought I had the right to witness the conversation that would take place in the kitchen.

However, my father said no. He preferred that I not be there. He asked if I would take round bales off a nearby field.

It was many years later that I learned the history that preceded that moment. In the early 2000s, my grandfather received a loan from M&T Bank to help ride out the low milk price at that time. It included a large balloon payment at the end, which would later be labeled predatory and made illegal. My grandfather knew that the terms were not fair, but he thought that he had no choice. He might have leaned on the old wisdom that milk prices ran in seven-year cycles. Regardless of those ups and downs, my grandfather's farm never caught up again. Instead, it started to accumulate debt.

My grandfather decided that he needed to borrow more money. Since this was several years after he hit his head, my father probably started to realize—before the rest of us did—that my grandfather wasn't as perceptive as he used to be. Keeping a farm operating through low prices takes moxie and skill, and my grandfather had done it many times before. However, seeking out a second loan was not only risky, but also a red flag. M&T was not going to loan my grandfather any more money, and because both farms were under the same mortgage, my father was liable for that loan, too, and therefore ineligible to be granted another one with the bank. Instead, my grandfather asked my father to take out a loan with the Farm Service Agency and give him the money.

Although I've done my best to pursue the story of our family, this is a moment where it falls into shadows. There was a conversation between my father and grandfather, and it will never be known what was said. Once, when I was an adult drinking gin with my father on the porch, he implied that there were certain things he couldn't tell me. He was bad at keeping secrets, so I knew that he had a reason and that I had to accept it. Perhaps he was talking about this loan. I wonder what my grandfather promised in exchange for this subterfuge, or if he insisted that it was necessary to keep the farm running until I could take it over. My father was an intelligent, discerning person who knew better than to sign those papers, but he also cared for my grandfather. In the end, it might have been love and not reason that convinced him to go along with the plan.

My father took out a loan of $200,000 and secretly gave it to my grandfather. The intent of the financing was for my father to purchase more cattle for his herd. As a trade for the $200,000, my grandfather gave him two injured heifers that were only good for beef.

A man named Bob Brennan oversaw my father's account at FSA. My parents went to his office for a meeting. Because FSA visited the farm regularly to check on its condition, it was reported that my father did not purchase any cattle with the $200,000. From what I know, the conversation went something like this:

Bob Brennan watched my parents sit down in his office and continued to stare at my father after he had taken his seat. Brennan was a similar age, with khakis and a polo shirt. Stationed behind a desk of paperwork, he did not look like a man who got upset often. However, on that day, the skin on his neck was red. Finally, he spoke.

"We have a problem, Derrick."

My father leaned forward and folded his hands. He bowed his head and nodded unconsciously.

When it was apparent that my father was not going to respond, Brennan put his palms on the desk and leaned back. "Where are the cows, Rick?"

My father cleared his throat. "Well," he said, staring at the carpet in front of him. "I haven't picked them all up yet. And part of that is that I've been so busy catching up on hay after the rain that I hadn't gotten a chance to look at a lot of cattle, and—"

Brennan raised his hands in the air. "I'm afraid we're going to need the money back."

My father started nodding again, his hands still clasped. He knew better than to look at my mother because she wasn't going to make eye contact with him. "The thing is," he said, "because I haven't had much chance to travel around seeing cattle, I ended up purchasing youngstock from Dad, with the agreement of more to come. Because I respect his breeding I—"

By this time my father realized that Brennan had stood up and was pointing his finger at him. He didn't wait for my father to finish because he probably already knew it was a lie. "This is fraud," Brennan said. "It's serious." He shifted on his feet but still held his finger out. "If I don't turn you in I could lose my job."

I don't know why, but Brennan took on that risk. He paced around the room, yelling at my father and telling him what a stupid thing he did as my father sat there quietly. Sometimes he pounded his desk with a fist as he went by. I imagine spit flying from his mouth and landing on top of his brown shoes. Finally, Brennan collapsed back into his chair. Then he let my parents leave, never telling anyone what my father had done.

As a teenager, I didn't know how difficult previous loan meetings had been for my father, nor what he had already taken on himself. To me, I was being sent away like a child. I didn't know that he had felt the same way once before. These meetings were vulnerable moments for him, and he didn't want anyone to see them who didn't have to, especially his children. I was already aware of how close to their chests the Dennis men kept the financial side of farming. What I didn't know was how heavy that burden was.

All Hail the New Adult

THERE'S A PLAQUE NEAR THE SCHOOL'S MAIN OFFICE. My name is on it three times for winning the science fair. I had an hourlong bus ride to and from the school each day, and I used it to do my homework. I was never sent to the principal. When no one's hand went up, I waited and then answered to save the teacher from silence. Every class had one or two students that the other kids called eggheads. I wouldn't have been smart or dedicated enough to be noticed in a larger place. However, Canaseraga Central School only graduated twenty-four students my senior year. I was valedictorian and therefore had to give a speech at the graduation ceremony.

Looking back, I'm not sure why I said what I did. Maybe I thought being the good kid meant being mundane and predictable, and I didn't want that pinned on me so easily as I prepared for the idea of a bigger world. I also didn't think graduation day was as significant as other people did. I've always had an aversion to traditions that are meant to be heavy with import. Weddings are fine until I run into the bride and groom and I'm supposed to say how nice they look and how special the ceremony was, instead of nodding my head and smiling awkwardly.

At the graduation rehearsal, the superintendent asked to review my speech. I told him I didn't have one: I just wanted to speak from the heart. He said he needed a speech to review, so I wrote down whatever the valedictorian was expected to say, talking about going into the future with courage and thanking those who had gotten us this far.

However, when it came time to address my family, classmates, and community, I didn't say those things. Instead, I tried to be funny. I said I wasn't going to thank anyone and then talked about how surviving

Canaseraga meant that whatever came next would be easy. Years later, I actually can't piece together much of my speech. I think my subconscious tried to suppress it. I have hazy memories of laughing faces, somewhat stunned; the green and white banners made in art classes; and a few paintings of Native Americans because our mascot was the Indian. Now, it feels like a hallucinatory movie montage with floating heads and carnival music. However, for my family, it was a very real moment in time, with my words echoing around the gym. Especially when I said, "Look at how far I've come, seeing what I've come from," and then pointed at my parents.

Afterwards, my mother, sister, and I waited next to our Pontiac for my father. My aunt Lydie, one of my biggest supporters, had found him on the way out of the gymnasium and called the spectacle shameful. I wasn't told about it until later. The ride home was quiet, though I didn't notice. As expected, I had won a handful of small scholarships, the rural school doing its best to support its graduates. I still had electricity in my veins from speaking in front of a crowd. The streetlamps buzzed as we drove through town, throwing light on my parents' stoic faces. Some aunts and uncles were meeting at the house afterwards for cake and ice cream. They ate quickly and went home. I assumed they were just tired, since it was getting late into the evening. By profession and nature, we were all early risers.

It wasn't until a day or two later, when I was making some self-congratulatory remark, that my father had finally had enough.

"Do you really want to know what we thought about your speech? Do you really want to know?" He got up from his seat and pointed his finger at me. "Your mother said she was never so embarrassed in her life."

Wearing a cap and gown was supposed to mark my entry into adulthood—and in a way, it did. Between the farm and school, I had always considered myself responsible. It never occurred to me that I could hurt anyone. Only later did I realize how hard it was for my parents not to say anything, still being willing to let me have a moment that came once in a lifetime. My father's formal education ended in high school. I didn't think of what the ceremony might have meant to him. Even more jarring was that I had snuck up on myself. I didn't see that part of me lurking in my subconscious until it was too late—until I had already made the wrong decision. It turns out, maybe I wasn't such a good kid after all.

The Chopper

Every morning my father and grandfather met at the trench.

If it was still cool out, a haze would lift off the silage and dissipate into the sunlight. Sometimes, when the first tractor pulled in, a woodchuck scurried out of one of the bays of the grain shed and disappeared into the weeds. We didn't eat breakfast at my grandparents' anymore, having less time to spare, so this is where my father and grandfather saw each other. Usually, my grandfather would be finishing loading his mixer wagon when my father arrived. While my father waited, he might, if it was needed, climb onto the pile of silage being fed out and pull back the plastic. The top layer always had the shape of the tires that held the plastic down. Emily rode in the loader tractor with my grandfather and stayed there in the corner when my father climbed in. Knowing the routine as well as anyone, she got there first to make sure she was lifted up the steps.

There were times when the shed bays held cottonseed or cornmeal, but most often we fed the cattle distillers' grain. It was golden colored and had a sweet smell. As a byproduct of whiskey production, it was usually cheaper. Every morning, birds crowded along the base of the pile. As children, my sister and I fell backwards into it with our arms spread.

When the mixer wagons were newer, my father and grandfather watched the scale readouts on the side of machine, but everything electrical eventually wore out. Instead, they learned how many bucketloads of silage and grain were needed, and roughly how full those buckets should be. They lowered the tractor's arms and drove into the silage until the pile pushed against them, and then tipped the bucket up and reversed, following the same ruts in the mud. If a tire slid off the plastic and fell into the silage, they stopped and pitched it to the side of the bank.

Once my grandfather had filled his mixer wagon with silage and grain, he climbed out of the loader tractor, holding the grab bar, and then waved. My father met him in the middle of the driveway and they both put their hands on their hips.

"What do you know today?" my grandfather always said.

More times than not he wore a colored polo shirt with stripes. I don't know if such shirts were popular with men from his generation or if my grandmother just kept buying them. The two men talked about the weather by saying, "What do you think it's going to do today?" If it was winter, my father would bring up the Bills' defense and say again, "Wouldn't it be good if we had a quarterback?" and my grandfather would say "Gawd" and purse his lips. They both had the habit of nodding their heads in silence and staring at the ground. If they got any news out of the milkman, they would share it. They might mention a sick cow if they had one or if something broke since the day before, and the other would ask if they needed a hand. Then they would plan what fields to work that day. My father would say, "What do you think, Boss?" and my grandfather would push his hands out in front of him and say, "I'm not the boss, you are." They would nod their heads for a while, until eventually someone said, "Well." Then they got back into their tractors.

In farming together for so long, a liturgy developed between the two men. It was a call-and-response that became natural. They carried it out, knowing the rest of their days were set, and they might have taken comfort in it. If all else changed around them, but what they did stayed the same, that was something to hold on to.

One day, however, my grandfather wasn't at the trench.

My father sat in the tractor for a few minutes. The radio played through the static and he sang along to parts of the lyrics. Brown felt drooped from the ceiling of the cab. My father reached his finger up to pin it back in place for a moment and then let it fall again, trying to remember once more to bring a few tacks from the house. He used the end of his shirt to rub the dust off the gauges on the dashboard and then held it out to study the smudges in the fabric. My father decided to drive the loader tractor to my grandparents' place. After the accident, he had all the justification he needed to check on my grandfather.

At the house, my grandmother said that my grandfather already had breakfast. She assumed that he was at the trench to load the mixer wagon.

My father drove the tractor out to the barn. The chopper was on its jack, pulled off to the side. Various wrenches lay in the grass around it. Behind the chopper stood bright green stalks of corn, their tassels swaying when there was a breeze. A sheet of aluminum had slid off the roof of the heifer section. It leaned against a pile of scrap metal in the weeds. A mound of manure and bedding had been pushed outside the calf barn. It collected at the base of a dead birch tree, bleak against the gray sky, and added an unnecessary gothic feel. My father would have cut it down for that alone, but without telling anyone the reason.

"You snooping around?" My grandfather's voice came from beneath the chopper. His work shoes emerged from under the snout as he inched himself out. My father grabbed his legs and pretended to pull, but my grandfather's hand slapped at him as my grandfather said, "Don't" and "Gawd."

My father grabbed him by the arm and pulled him to his feet. He dusted off my grandfather's jeans like a child, further teasing him.

"What, did you forget you had cows to feed?" my father said.

"They're not worried, why should you be?"

My father slowly lowered himself into the grass and then lay on his side to look at the undercarriage of the chopper. He ran his fingers along some corroded bolt threads. "You haven't called a dealer yet."

"Charlie's man looked at it and said they couldn't do anything with it."

"A dealer who could fix it," my father said, picking a few sockets out of the grass and piling them together. The bolts where the knives met the cutter bar had worn away and the machine could not cut properly. There wasn't access to get where the bolts had to be changed. The corn needed to be chopped soon. Most the year's forage was still standing.

"You can be under there until you rot and it won't make much difference," my father said.

My grandfather lifted his hand to motion towards the barn. "See if you can find a five-eighths on the desk. I looked, but your eyes are better than mine." His knuckles were bleeding. He rubbed them on the side of his shirt and left a streak.

If my father thought about telling my grandfather to look himself, he wouldn't have considered it for long. He would have found it less of a hassle to grab a wrench than to get into conflict. What's more, he had lived his whole life deferring to my grandfather, who was not only his father, but a farmer he respected. He stopped at the door of the barn and was about to slide it open when he noticed it was missing one of its rollers. He jiggled it back and forth as he examined it. "Want me to find you some screws too?"

My grandfather was sorting through the tools in the grass, trying to find the right socket extension.

Inside, my father reached for the light switch but found that it didn't work. Paper towels used for milking overflowed the garbage can and a pile of netwrap filled up one corner. Despite the manure outside, the calf section still needed cleaning. A half cup of coffee sat in the sink where the calf buckets were washed. Something compelled my father to pick it up and smell it. "Christ," he whispered, and dumped it.

My father kicked the weeds outside the barn until he found the roller and then placed it just inside the door. My grandfather had his arms folded, staring at the chopper. My father held the wrench out for a while before my grandfather noticed it. "We can find a dealer who can get at the cutter bar," my father said. "We just need to look further than Canaseraga."

"We'll get it." My grandfather headed towards his freestall barn, where his mixer wagon was parked.

"If Charlie's mechanics couldn't fix it, how can we? It makes no sense," my father said. "I'll look around."

"No," my grandfather said. He stopped suddenly. "It'd be expensive and a waste of time."

"The corn is about ready. We can't fuck around anymore."

The two men faced each other in the driveway. The skin on my grandfather's neck was red under his tan. He eventually folded his arms and lowered his head, a posture associated with contemplation, but for my grandfather meant that he was fixing himself in place. Instead, my father's shoulders immediately softened. He exhaled slowly, through the nose. He fell to nodding his head, unconsciously.

There weren't many times in his life that my father raised his voice to my grandfather. I wasn't there that day, and I hadn't seen it before. However, I can picture my grandfather standing there, looking at the ground. My father knew better than anyone that if he hadn't responded by then, he wasn't going to. My father stared at him in the silence.

"Just doesn't make sense," my father said, climbing into his tractor. He shut the door and turned the key, lifting exhaust into the air.

Beyond the Hill

It wasn't until hours of flat cornfields passed by the window of the Greyhound bus that I realized I had pictured the entire world hilly and full of trees like Canaseraga.

The first time I lived away from the farm was to study English and biology at Alfred State, a two-year college fourteen miles away. I roomed with one of my classmates from Canaseraga and we cooked venison in our dorm room on a George Foreman grill. We befriended a forty-year-old man with a handlebar mustache and intense eyes named Crazy Karl, because he could buy us beer. I joined the dairy judging team, and we got funding from the college to go to the large cattle show in Toronto but instead went to the strip clubs on Yonge Street.

At Alfred State, I met a professor who took me under his wing to teach me writing. He was a farmer's son himself, and that might have had something to do with agreeing to meet me every week to review my work. Soon after, he pointed out that I used improper verb forms, such as *I seen* and *he done*. He suggested that it was important that I fix this in order to be taken seriously. It was the first time that I looked the short distance back to the place I came from.

A year later, I transferred to the University of Iowa, a thousand miles away. Something about being on a bus suited me. It was a similar type of contemplation and endurance as sitting in a tractor cab. Watching the landscape change helped me understand what was in front of me. Iowa City was, by name and size, an actual city, with 60,000 citizens. That made it 120 times larger than Canaseraga.

I ended up living in what used to be an old boardinghouse, taking one of its twelve rooms. A man in his sixties named Steve lived in the basement. He was heavy-built with a white beard and a purple beret. My first night after moving in, he invited me downstairs. The first thing I noticed when I descended the steps was that his mattress was propped off the ground by rows of Ten High bottles. He drank from a fifth but offered it to me often. Before the night was over, the bottle was empty. More notably, by then he had duct-taped me to a chair, ripped my shirt open with an army knife, and pointed a loaded pistol at my head. He was laughing, so I knew it was in jest. In the end, I wasn't alarmed and didn't resist much. This was the city. This was apparently what city people did.

Those in farming families are expected to take what has been given to them and pass it on. It makes them part of a continuum of land, cattle, and history that preceded their existence and is meant to outlive them. Going to Iowa was the first major event that was outside of that script, which made it my own. No one in my family, as far as I knew, had ever been to Iowa. I had put my own imprint on my life. It turned out, Steve drank a bottle of whiskey every night and was glad for the company. He gave me Ten High and meatloaf and introduced me to some of the artists and writers in the city. He could charm anyone, sometimes by making his shorts fall down on cue. Occasionally, he had me hold a door open so he could ride his bike through a bar. A few times we had to cycle away from cops. My father had told me about being wild in high school, the anecdotes stopping at the age of seventeen when he got his own farm. Now this was my window to create stories that I would tell for the rest of my life, building a narrative that I had chosen for myself.

Still, none of it really mattered. I was out in the world, in a city among city people, but I knew the farm still stood in Canaseraga. It was there to protect who I really was. I felt it—in the difficulty of sleeping late no matter when I went to bed, or the sudden anxiety around four o'clock, for a moment thinking it was time to do calf chores before realizing that there were no calf chores for me in Iowa. I was on a break from all that, playing with house money before having to go back and take my place in what I was supposed to do.

One day I walked into the International Office on campus. Since I was billed for out-of-state tuition, going out of the country didn't cost any more. I had studied Spanish in high school but couldn't imagine relying on it. A bearded man sat behind a desk, and I told him I wanted to go to Ireland. He said that he had just gotten back from Galway, and he loved it. The University of Iowa didn't have an exchange program there, but he said we could work around that.

The first thing I noticed in Ireland was the cars parked on the sidewalk. All the streets were lined with vehicles that had two wheels on the walkway, because the roads themselves were so narrow. I suddenly realized that there wasn't anything wrong with allowing cars to park on the sidewalk, only that I had never thought of it before.

Once I found a place to live, I put a large road map of the island on my wall. I had one semester there before returning to Iowa for my last year of college. Every weekend, I hopped onto Bus Éireann and went to another town. Before, most of my days had been spent in a tractor cab, with only my thoughts and an old border collie, so I didn't mind traveling alone. Some trips I took with a small group of international students. Once I went to Dublin with another American. Because we couldn't find a hostel to sleep in, we walked the streets all night, with various strangers who took ecstasy, climbed lampposts, and went to clubs. Another time, I found myself stranded in Derry, where there were no hostels and where buses only ran a few times a week. I was traveling with another student, and we decided to walk through the night, to Cardonagh, thirty kilometers away. At one point, we tried to lie down in a field and sleep for an hour, but because it was cold, we had to keep going. It was the first time I smoked pot, because anything might as well have happened that night.

Ireland felt full of possibility. I could talk to anyone, anytime, and many nights in new towns were spent having long conversations with old men I couldn't understand. I ended up anywhere from drinking with other farmers' sons to traveling on a band's tour bus. A few weeks before my classes began, I decided to take a trip to Belfast. I dropped my bag off at the hostel and wandered the streets.

"You got a fag?" a guy asked me. He was about my age, with a shaved head, suspenders over a white shirt, and tattoos on his neck and arms.

I told him I hadn't started smoking yet, but that someday I would. It was a dumb joke that I used too often. Instead of laughing, he froze.

"You're a Yank, aren't you? You're coming with me."

He took me by the shirt collar and pulled me across the street. Traffic screeched to a halt in front of us.

"Name's Matt," he said. He shook my hand as he dragged me along.

He explained to me the difference between *mate* and *cunt* in Ireland and said that even though in America you can't say *cunt*, in Ireland it means mate and if someone called you mate you better knock their block off before they do the same to you. It was only nine at night on a busy street and he wasn't much bigger than me. I could have caused a scene and gotten away, but I always had a problem with disappointing people.

"Do I sound aggressive to you, Yank?"

"No," I said, politely.

"They say Belfast has an aggressive accent. How you doing, mate?"

He laughed and slapped me on the back with his free hand.

The place was called Writer's Square, in the middle of the city. There were about thirty kids dressed in black, most of them younger than us. They skateboarded, smoked pot, played soccer, burned things, and ran into walls. They had piercings and tattoos and some of them wore

Carhartt jackets, eyeing me with suspicion. They were, at least informally, the punks of Belfast.

"Hey, everyone," Matt shouted. "I found a Yank!"

They came up and circled me, sniffing my clothes. One girl said that all Americans smelled the same.

"How's that?" I asked.

"Musty."

Matt was the oldest one there. Whatever his appearance used to be, he dressed in lighter-colored clothes and with less tatter. Only by standing next to me did he seem more punkish. That might have been in the back of his mind when he grabbed me.

A punk asked me if I liked the band Tool. Before I could answer she slipped a headset over my ears. The music was loud and fast with a throaty electric guitar. I couldn't figure out what the singer was shouting.

"Good stuff," I said.

Another kid put his arm over my shoulder and with Buckfast on his breath told me how the Troubles were simply about nationalism and never about religion. "No one is going to throw a bomb at you because you didn't go to mass," he said. "It was an excuse Britain made up for the rest of the world, to keep the six counties, like." Other kids joined in to tell the next story, which was about a pedophile who had lived in Belfast. A group of concerned citizens, they said—and here they deviously snickered—showed up at the door and asked for his ID. Then they took him out to the shed where he had abused the girl. They nailed his genitals to a sawhorse, doused him in petrol, handed him a hacksaw, and then lit a match.

"He had a choice, you know!" Matt said, laughing into the night.

At one point they decided they were going to someone's house on the edge of town. "Come on, Yank," Matt said, putting his arm around me and leading me away.

Another punk stepped in front of us. "I'm sorry man," he said, addressing me. "You're sound and all, but it's probably not a good idea. You're sound, you know, but . . ." He used the silence to indicate that I wasn't really one of them, made apparent by the way I looked and how I talked.

I wondered if Matt was going to be told something similar one day. He could have days hanging out with this crowd, or maybe years, and probably he didn't know himself what he was going to do. Maybe he got a nine-to-five and became somebody's neighbor. Maybe he has kids of his own and hides his tattoos under his shirt sleeves. He could have fallen into a personal crisis and found the life ahead tough. Part of coming of age is having to reconcile the world beyond us. What happens to anyone when they are forced to move on from the person they were?

"Well, I'm off then, mate," Matt said. He looked at me, grinned with a squinted eye, and tossed a Buckfast bottle into the night sky behind him. It shattered somewhere on the pavement. Then he, too, walked into the darkness. I thought I heard him laugh and yell, "See you, Yank!" before he disappeared, becoming a shadow, and then nothing at all.

It could have been that night, or all the other small moments adding up since I left for college, but at some point, a line ran through me. Until then, I had lived in the consistency of a field, going up and down it, season to season, and in the daily pattern of milking and feeding, with the steady pulse of the milkers. These rhythms reinforced me and my family. They were the netting that held our identity together. Against that uniformity, however, a different place or a new person was a grand experience. I often sat on a bench behind the Galway campus and looked at all the distinct details—stone walls, bright grass, small cars. There was a statue—a gift from the queen—that they put behind the Quadrangle and out of view, and it fascinated me that this place was formed from an entirely different history. To be enthralled by a different culture was a cliché, and I hated that part of it, but it still had a hold on me. Everything beyond how I grew up lay ahead and latent, unexplored. It was an awareness difficult to ignore.

On the Hood of a Chevy

Riding to the bus stop, my father and I were quiet. Eventually he turned on the radio. While we were both probably glad for the noise, it also felt like a surrender. I had been going back to college in Iowa for several years now, and each time, the day was marked by a strange nervousness. I eventually learned to name the feeling guilt.

The Greyhound left from a gas station twelve miles from Canaseraga. The roads and streets were familiar; I had driven through them hundreds of times, but I was aware that they would look a little different when I got back. The time that would pass until then felt like loss. There was dried mud on the seat of the Chevy, and it was probably going to rub into my jeans. Instead of scrubbing it out, I would have stared at it on the bus.

"Have your wallet?" my father asked again.

Every time I packed to leave, he tried to give me things. He always inquired if I had enough money, and when I wouldn't take any, he tried to hand me random items like a package of socks he hadn't opened yet or the sunglasses on his head. Once he put a Phillips screwdriver in my bag just in case I needed it in Iowa.

He parked the truck around the corner of the pumps. We watched locals pull in, fill up their vehicles, and leave. Because it was a larger town, there was a mix of people and we didn't know any of them. My father had done a lot for me through the years. He had prioritized being a good parent. I realized that this was a moment to give something back to him, but I didn't know what it was. Watching him over my lifetime, I knew that sons had to do things for their fathers sometimes. I just didn't know how.

Every time I left, it materialized my father's fear that I would decide not to stay on the farm. Going back to Iowa showed him what that day would look like.

When the bus pulled in, he embraced me silently and then I showed my ticket to the driver. He opened the luggage hatch so I could put my bag into the undercarriage. I took a seat by the window and looked to see if my father was going to watch the bus pull away, but his truck had already turned onto the street. I pushed my backpack between my legs and then put my foot through the strap, in case someone tried to take it when I fell asleep. Only a few people had gotten on at this stop and they were heading to Rochester or Buffalo, the closest cities. The fabric on the seatbacks in front of me was stained. It had someone's initials scratched in it with a knife. I took a book out of my bag and left it in my lap, but for now rested my head on the glass.

When the Greyhound departed, it went back through the town the same way my father and I did to get there. Although I had just seen the houses and storefronts along the route, they suddenly looked different from the height of a bus heading a thousand miles away. Because this town was big enough to have a Walmart and a few restaurants, we often went there to eat or do our own shopping. It was familiar and we had a connection to it, but it didn't feel like ours. Still, I looked out at the last buildings I recognized before settling into the long journey.

Through the dusty window, my father's red Chevy caught my eye. It was in a parking lot off the road, in front of a hairdresser's and wholesale chicken store. The lot was vacant in the late morning, and the white lines were mostly faded.

My father leaned over the Chevy's hood, crying.

Intervention

Aunt Lydie and Uncle John took to traveling in their retirement. They would rarely be home for long before once more going back and forth across the United States to visit friends and relatives. They saw a cousin on the West Coast while I was in my last semester at the University of Iowa. They decided to stop in Iowa City on their way back.

Other than my mother, who rode with me on the Amtrak to visit the university before I started classes, no one from the adolescence I left behind had seen my college existence. Iowa City was a thousand miles from Canaseraga; it felt like a whole other world that I had made for myself.

Achievement was important to Aunt Lydie and Uncle John, and they liked the fact that I had done well in school. They often took me out to dinner and told me they were proud of me.

When they called to say that they would soon be in Iowa City, they told me to pick out a restaurant. I chose Formosa because it was a place that I couldn't afford myself and wouldn't get to try otherwise. However, when the waitress placed a dish of peapods in front of us for an appetizer, I suddenly felt ashamed. Our meals were small and not particularly satisfying. Out of politeness, my aunt and uncle didn't say anything. I wanted to apologize and say that those peapods didn't indicate what I thought of myself.

On the walk back to my room, we passed through the cobblestone pedestrian street, filled with college kids and eccentrics lounging in the sun. It was the same place where, at night, I would watch Steve drink Ten High from his prescription bottle and yell to college boys that he would fight them for their women. I gave my aunt and uncle what local history I could, and when that ran out, I pointed at which bars I sometimes went in. A girl approached us with a yellow flyer and told us that Obama was going to speak there tomorrow. Uncle John leaned towards her and said, "Who cares?" Then, realizing that he had probably been too harsh, said, "My nephew would like to see him." He took the leaflet from her hand and held it to my chest.

I probably should have sensed that there was more that they wanted to tell me that afternoon, but I am not always the best at picking up such things. It would be years before I could read the weather in a room. If I had an inkling before, it would have dissipated as they left me at the old white house I lived in and headed down the sidewalk.

I flopped onto my bed, grabbing whatever required reading for my next English class was within reach. I had made it through a few pages by the time there was a knock on my door. I opened it and found Aunt Lydie standing in front of me.

"Ryan," she said, a bit breathless and agitated. "We don't think you should take over the farm."

Like every college student, I was constantly asked what I was going to do when I graduated. I told the people in Iowa, Ireland, and outside my family that I was planning to take over my grandfather's farm. Once in a while, the listener would be candid and reply with something like, "That's going to be tough." However, no one before had told me not to do it. They didn't plainly say that it would be a bad decision and a waste of education.

Depending on the day he was asked, my father described the end of his youth differently. He had called it a tremendous opportunity, getting set up with his own farm when he was only seventeen. In other moments though, quieter ones when he had turned reflective and might have been on the porch with a glass of gin in his hand, he lamented that he never got to go to college. He was fourth in his class by grades, but for his generation there was little doubt that the sons of farmers and business owners would become farmers and business owners themselves. Once, he said that he wanted to go into the Air Force but couldn't because of the farm, although he never admitted that again. He would have been a calm and reliable pilot, the type someone would want to fly with. However, he was also good at farming. He enjoyed it and did well with what was given to him, although he didn't arrive at that place in life by his own volition. Sometimes, in my worst moments, I wondered if he wasn't better off for not having a choice.

"Thank you for your opinion," I said, my face getting hot. "It's my decision to make." I still gripped the door handle in one hand.

My aunt stood on the porch, staring down the street and nodding her head. Students passed by on the sidewalk, some of them in school colors, their laughter fading behind them. The campus bus exhaled as it came to a stop, and when no one got out, turned into traffic again. Across the street, a girl locked her bicycle to a street sign. She was digging through her backpack when she disappeared into a university building. Eventually my aunt reached up and touched my arm. She smiled, looking at me intently. Then she carefully descended the steps, one foot at a time, and started the long journey towards home.

Smelling Smoke

Their living room faced Canaseraga, so my grandmother saw the fire trucks coming.

She sat on the couch and my grandfather in his chair while they watched soapies. After *The Young and Restless* was over, *As the World Turns* started before the commercial break, and then later *Guiding Light*. Whenever I had lunch there, I asked them what had changed since I last visited. My grandmother would shake her head and tell me who was sleeping with who now. "God," she'd say, almost stretching the vowel like my grandfather did. My grandfather would drift in and out of sleep. My grandmother yelled "Andy!" whenever he snored too loud.

My grandfather always fell asleep in the chair, even at Easter and Christmas. When my father got into his late thirties, he did the same. Having to get up early to milk, a small nap after lunch was probably necessary. Years later, I would be told about my grandfather's drinking, but I never noticed it myself. He was discrete enough that my sister and I were never aware of it. However much his drinking might have affected his day-to-day life, it was masked by a greater change in his behavior.

There weren't many places past my grandparents' that would be in the fire company's remit. My grandmother heard the trucks shift gears and slow down before their mailbox. Her first assumption would be that a dry cow was out and standing in the road. Then the trucks passed by the window again, bouncing down the driveway. The sun glared off their bright red paint as they slowed down for the ruts and puddles, but still went fast enough to show urgency. I wasn't there, but I can imagine my grandmother standing behind the sliding glass door with her arms folded, staring at the large vehicles.

"Andy!"

My grandfather had to clear old silage from the bunker behind his house. Instead of bucketing it out and spreading it on the fields, he decided to take a shortcut: he poured diesel fuel over it and set it on fire. After he got the blaze going, he went back to his armchair and fell asleep. He didn't take the time to pull out the trench plastic and old tires on top of the silage. Once they caught flame, they created a column of black smoke that rose into the sky. Presumably whoever called the fire department had tried to call my grandfather first, but he had stopped answering the phone because of bill collectors. Instead, he slept in the chair as a parade of fire trucks rolled by his living room.

It didn't seem like we talked about my grandfather's deterioration often, although it might have been something my parents discussed without my sister and me. It probably crept into conversations my parents had in the quiet of night. The few times my father had to explain it to someone outside of the family, he would just say, "He's getting older," and allow the other person to work out what that meant. Because my grandfather had helped my father purchase his farm from Clair, both farms were under the same mortgage. It is a sad phenomenon when parents or grandparents struggle as they age, but if they are running a farm—one whose finances are connected to your livelihood—then it becomes more than a natural process that one must learn to accept. Instead, it is farm business, and farm business is kept private.

Maybe it was competition between brothers, or the effect of falling out with his father after returning to the home farm, but my grandfather—who was once jovial and quick to fall back on humor—was also not afraid to act boldly to get his way. One Christmas, before his accident, our family sat in the living room after opening presents. Half-filled coffee cups and plates with cookie crumbs were on the table and the carpet next to the couch. Jeff, Kelly's husband, still sat on the floor next to the tree, having helped hand out presents. He balled up some crinkled wrapping paper and threw it at my aunt. They hadn't been married for very long. Then he turned to my grandfather.

"Andy, can I borrow a bull off you? I have some heifers that didn't catch."

My grandfather sat in his armchair, staring straight ahead. He didn't look at Jeff nor signal that anything had been said out loud, even though we all heard it.

Jeff looked at the rest of us, as if trying to find an explanation for the sustained silence. It was apparent to us that my grandfather did not want to lend out a bull.

The ploy worked, because Jeff never asked again.

My grandfather became quiet and aloof after the accident, but in a way that wasn't calculated. His old urge towards humor sometimes surfaced, but it didn't always make sense. More than once, he asked if I kissed guys before I dated them, the insinuation being that I must be gay since I never brought a girl to meet him. Those types of comments bothered my father more than me, but he never reprimanded my grandfather, at least not in front of anyone. It was a small thing to have to accept. Similarly, when my grandfather called our house to ask me to put a bale into his dry cows, even though he could have done it himself, it was mostly harmless. He was a man used to being in control, and these small requests helped him feel like he still had some.

It was a trait of Dennis men to tell stories, in the polite way that means to exaggerate. The tales my grandfather started to tell, however, were getting more difficult to believe. He said he once saw a turkey buzzard pick up a live calf and take it away. He would follow up such statements by saying he had never seen such a thing in all his years of farming. Another time, he said that people were infecting our pond with a special type of algae out of malice. Once, he said that my father was having an affair with a woman up the road, even though that woman had moved away twenty years ago. Not everything my grandfather said could be shrugged away so easily, however. In addition to all the things he had never seen before in all his years of farming, Andy Dennis had another mantra: "I don't pay liens."

The loader tractor was not the last bill he fell behind on. He had to switch feed companies several times after each one stopped extending credit. Other services and contractors, from mechanics to fuel companies, had outstanding invoices that were never settled. My grandfather frequently received letters and then phone calls from their lawyers, some of which threatened to throw him in jail. It was all easy for him to shake off. Whether it was a legal representative on the phone or my father standing in front of him, he'd scrunch his face, push his hands out, and say, "I don't pay liens."

It's very likely that my grandfather told M&T Bank, which held the combined mortgage on his and my parents' farm, his position on liens. The year before, in the summer of 2006, the price of milk dropped to nearly ten dollars a hundredweight, almost half of what it had been in the summer of 2004. During this time, the value of a dairy cow essentially halved, falling to about $1,000 for a bred two-year-old. Hence, the value of a farmer's assets on the balance sheet was suddenly lower. However, my grandfather kept demanding to borrow more money to catch up, even though that would not solve the problem, and the bank had refused to lend it. Maybe my grandfather was persistent, or in their regular meetings, they saw how difficult it was for him to understand his circumstances. Either way, the bank realized what we had already known: my grandfather was no longer rational. M&T Bank asked my father to seek power of attorney.

One of the cruelest aspects of my grandfather's head injury was that he no longer had the will to farm. I don't know what his reality felt like after the accident, but he lost the clarity he needed to handle what was before him, and after that, the resolve to try. As might be the case with many brain injuries, he knew that something wasn't right inside him, but he couldn't fix himself. As a result, he was increasingly estranged from what mattered most to him. I don't know how often he put Black Velvet in his coffee or if my grandmother knew about it, but the daily rhythms of the milking parlor and the field started to vex him.

In the end, my father did not seek power of attorney. The reasons, when explained, would vary through the years. Sometimes my father said that it would have killed my grandfather. He was already starting to disconnect from life, and it might have extinguished what volition was left. Other times, it was out of general respect. My father remembered my grandfather being a farmer ahead of his time and giving my father a start in the business. It would have been hard and complicated for the family if my father tried to get power of attorney over my grandfather. He probably wanted to avoid the drama for all of us.

Instead, my grandfather carried on. We laughed at how he pretended not to hear questions that he didn't want to answer, but, eventually, ignoring problems became his strategy for dealing with them.

When I was home, I'd visit my grandparents often. My grandmother enjoyed my company, and every few days called to say that she had just taken something out of the oven. Once, I was eating at the table when a friendly-looking middle-aged man approached the sliding glass door with a manilla envelope.

My grandfather pulled the door open, greeting him. He probably thought it was someone asking to hunt on our land or a neighbor he forgot he met.

"Andrew Dennis?"

When my grandfather took the envelope, the man's smile faded. "You've been subpoenaed."

My grandmother watched the truck pull out of the driveway. Then she called my father. My grandfather simply tossed the packet of documents on the table and sat back down to watch soapies.

The Day I Was Asked

THE HEIFERS LEANED OVER THE FENCE, watching us drive in. Some of them shifted on their front hooves, knowing they were going to be fed.

It was a sunny day and there wasn't much snow on the ground. The shed roofs cast a wet glare. We had finished the morning milking, and our clothes still carried iodine and cow shit in them. We had several groups of heifers at Stonen Farms—outbuildings between my father's and grandfather's barns that were once owned by a newspaper baron who raised beefalo as a tax write-off. Like many of our fields, we called them by the history that predates us. We took a bucket full of pellets with the loader tractor, threw some five-gallon pails over the feed and drove up the hill, my father and I squeezed together in the cab.

Knowing my father, I think that he had waited until after Christmas to keep the holidays from getting ruined, and then a few weeks after that to make sure whatever happened couldn't be connected back to the Christmas season and taint it by association. It was a tough thing to ask because of everything behind it, and because he was probably afraid of the answer I was going to give.

We pulled open the door of the main shed, sending stray cats scattering behind the machinery. In some lots, we could reach over the wooden walls along the alley and dump the feed in, but for others we had to open the gate and carry the buckets to the mangers. We waded through the mud, our boot prints left behind us. Heifers crowded us and ate directly from the pails as quickly as they could, trying to use the bridge of their noses to yank the buckets out of our grasp. We poured the grain over their heads as they clamored above the troughs, some of it falling to the plastic with a hail-like patter, some of it getting stuck in the hair on the heifers' necks.

My father turned to me very suddenly and said, "Are you going to take over Grandpa's farm?"

This moment lingered around my father for years, all of it leading to this day. He probably couldn't help thinking about it in quiet hours. Its weight would have settled over him during the last few weeks. He would have carried it through the morning milking, through chores, and whether or not I knew it at the time, it filled the space of the tractor cab on the way to Stonen Farms.

I don't know if I stopped moving or not, but I was frozen. Stuck. As much as I tried to deny it, I knew the question was going to find me after coming back from university. The closest thing I had to a feeling was a glaring numbness that detached me from the moment. It was as if I was able to suddenly look at myself from somewhere else. Although I could barely hear whatever I mumbled, it was something about not knowing how to decide or being afraid of no longer developing as a person.

My father thrust a pail into the grain inside the tractor bucket and pulled it out, spilling pellets on the ground. He did the same for the other bucket. "Well, this is just a great day," he said, carrying the pails to the next group of heifers.

We rode back to the house in silence. Our arms carried the smell of feed dust, and my jeans had mucus from a heifer's nose. I stared out the tractor's dusty window at the tire turning below me. I looked past my reflection, ignoring that it was staring back at me.

The Weather in Canaseraga

In the morning, we walked to the barn in the dark. The snow on the ground had refrozen overnight and all the steps we had taken since the last flurries were spread before us, hardened. We had to be careful walking over them so we didn't fall. The wind blew whatever snow hadn't settled along the ground. We passed in and then out of the static of the dusk-to-dawn light. When we reached the barn, we got the cows from the freestalls.

In the parlor the milkers spread around us and, in the absence of much conversation, pulsated louder. The cattle stood in the holding area and exhaled pale mist as they chewed their cuds. Their body heat fogged the windows. They walked into the parlor to be milked in the same order they usually did, routine being as comforting to beasts as it is to man. My father did not ignore me, but there wasn't much he could say. We both knew it. Still, my father remaining quiet was worse than anything he could have said.

After milking, I wandered through the barn if I knew no one else was around. The calves kept in the old tiestalls lay in the hay beneath them, mostly settled after being fed. A few of them jumped to their feet when I passed, stretching their loins and curling their tails. A couple of the friendlier cats trotted over and rubbed against my boots, but I stepped past them. The blades of the fan built into the block wall slowly turned, pushed by air moving through the opening. It was a long time since they had electricity and gave comfort to the cattle once milked there. Often, I would linger. Sometimes I put my foot on the bottom rung of the sick pen and stared at whatever cow was there without really seeing her.

Yellow eyes stared from the shadows. They held me steady without flinching. My sister raised goats for 4-H as a teenager, but that was over ten years earlier. The doe was covered in burdock and a long mat hung off her chin. She let me try to pull apart the burrs for a minute or two before she stepped out of reach. Somehow, this goat had remained after my sister went to college, and it was impossible to keep her penned in. Eventually everyone gave up, and the goat lived free.

The goat usually slept in the old tiestall barn. At first, she watched us from its corners, always lurking within sight. Sometimes she snorted, tossed her head, and took a few steps closer. If I walked towards her and tried to touch her, she would dart away, still wary of being caught. Sometimes, she kicked up her legs and ran out of the barn for no apparent reason.

Now, the goat came out every time I was home and near the barn. I didn't know if she remembered me or was only glad for the company. I scratched her ears and let her rub her head on my pant legs. Maybe I was glad for the company, too.

Mostly the goat wanted me to put my hand out so she could rub the top of her head on it. Dust and dried skin flung from her scalp when she did this. She was thin and sometimes shook on cold days. Sometimes she would chase the cats for entertainment or butt at the calves to make them unsettled. Mostly, though, she walked through the shadows of the tiestall barn, her gothic mansion.

I suddenly felt disconnected from milking cattle and packing trench and all the other things I had done. That adolescence now belonged to some other person. That person would have taken over his grandfather's farm and pressed on with what was laid before him. The last coat of whitewash from the open house had started chipping off the walls. The concrete floor was covered in the hay we had dragged to the heifer pens. The chaff was dusty and concealed old syringes, cat bones, the broken shards of buckets, and other things lost inside it. Stained mugs sat on top of the fan in front of the parlor because I often forgot to take my empty coffee cups back with me to the house. Eventually my father would put them all in a calf bucket and bring them inside when he went for breakfast. He pretended to be annoyed, but I think he enjoyed the familiarity of the ritual. That day, I realized that a barn is as much a narrative as it is a place for cattle. Suddenly, I didn't know how to be in the world, nor if I had a place in it.

February is the worst time of year in New York State. After the Super Bowl, there is a long stretch of cold weather until spring and not much to look forward to. By then, the snow on the ground has grown dirty. Most people are tired of trudging through it.

It was an uneventful week at home. I was conscious of making an appearance in the living room or at the kitchen table, or to sit in front of a program that my parents were watching just to show that I wasn't hiding. We didn't talk much, especially about what was in front of us. I would have been better off if I could have said out loud why I didn't commit to taking over Grandpa Dennis's farm. Maybe my parents would have been better off for it, too. My mother knew well the sacrifices of living on a farm, particularly in terms of a career or education. I think she had supported my choice, or at least understood it. I think my father also discerned, at least in part, the complexity of the decision I was asked to make. By nature, he wouldn't try to impose his will on others, but even with everything that was at stake for the family, he never tried to push me to change my mind. I was twenty-three and should have had it in me to thank him for that. Instead, I folded into myself. I couldn't see past the fact that I had disappointed my family again, and in the biggest way I knew.

My father and I were feeding bottles to calves in the front pen of the tiestall barn. It usually took calves a few days to learn to drink from the bucket, and until then we used a nipple. I carried my intentions during the morning milking, trying to get the courage to tell them to my father.

I kept putting the conversation off with strained small talk or by accepting the awkward silence between us. The calves butted at the nipple, their tails swinging wildly. If our grip softened too much, they would knock the bottle out of our hands.

I turned to my father and said, "I'm going back to Iowa. Next week."

The calf my father fed jerked back and then searched for the nipple again with a gaping mouth. My father's face did not change. That was the way he took hard news. The calf finished the bottle and then the bottle gasped repeatedly as the calf sucked in air. My father pulled the nipple from its lips. "Do you think that's a good idea?" he said. That was the only thing he would say before returning to the milk house to wash the bottle.

I didn't have a way to justify it. I had no job there, nor a place to live. And I couldn't say the plain truth, which was that I couldn't stay at home and shoulder the guilt I felt. Instead, I needed those thousand miles.

Iowa City was the only other place I knew in the United States. There were things there that I enjoyed, like going to author readings, meeting the eccentrics of the city, and listening to Ace of Base. For the first time in my life, I had a gang, a group of four of us who went out together most days of the week. It might have been the first time that I really needed friends. While I was home in Canaseraga, I heard "The Sign" on the radio four times in one day and decided that must have been the sign itself. I drove to the gas station and bought a bus ticket.

I left home on February 22, 2008. Although I had made the same trip six or seven times before, this journey was different. By the time I arrived at the Iowa City terminal twenty-four hours later, the division inside me was final. I was a person who was born on a farm and I was someone who left it. The second person was new to the world and had a lot to think about. What began on an Irish sidewalk half-crowded by cars was now fully realized beneath a gray February sky, the white line passing by the bus tires.

Steve tried to set me up in an apartment owned by a woman named Laurie. Her husband, however, was a mean drunk who didn't care to take on freeloaders. Steve suggested that I work in the restaurant that Laurie owned downstairs. I was immediately inserted into a hectic atmosphere and given small tasks without much instruction. Nonetheless, after an hour of picking up water glasses too close to their rims and mostly standing around awkwardly, I was relieved of my duty and sent to live with Laurie's mother, Diane, who didn't charge me rent.

I got a minimum-wage job in a box factory. I called it "a box factory" because it was in a warehouse and we moved boxes around. In truth, it was the Pearson test-score center, where we received the exams taken by students all over the country and then sent them somewhere else. Growing up, every child hears some version of the same morality tale: a young person does not follow their parents' advice and makes the wrong decision and, as a result, fails to reach their full potential. I wondered if I would be the example given to the next generation in Canaseraga. Still, it was work, and this was the first time I got paid for it. When I saved $500, I applied for a master's in writing back in Galway.

My father told my grandfather that I needed to get an education before taking over his farm. That was why they waited until I had my undergraduate degree before asking me what I was going to do. Now that I was no longer that farmer's son working towards his own herd, I didn't have a story anymore. I wasn't part of any narrative. Continuing my studies was less about getting a higher degree than finding something to do that I could answer for. I tried to patch the pieces together into something that made sense.

In that absence, I learned that the rhythm of farming is carried with someone wherever they go. The pulse of the day, all the milkings and feedings, were still in me. Before, I had felt more capable than other people because I could do the same thing all week long, without days off. I was in sync with something greater than common needs. However, when there were no calves to feed or cows to milk, the alignment was wrong. It made the world seem foreign. In the tractor cab, I used to dream about what I could do if I had time to myself. I imagined that I could accomplish just about anything—write a book, compose music, start a political career—with the chance to work at it. Now, having it, time became oppressive and proved me to be ordinary.

Iowa City didn't have open land, but instead college greens, parking lots, and public parks. The sounds beyond my window were traffic and not restless cattle. When I went outside, any space I occupied had already, the same day, been passed through by hundreds of other people. I often stared at the small rectangles of grass between the sidewalk and someone's front porch. People went by with small dogs that stopped to smell the urine of other dogs. The park benches were scratched with names and it mattered less that I didn't know them than that no one else did, either. I walked through the city even if it was raining. By the time it stopped, crushed worms lay on the concrete. To some extent, we're kept by the things we see around us, and I didn't have a stake in any of it.

It was a while before I called home. The conversation would have been general and fact-based. I would have been told about the weather in Canaseraga. I didn't have much to report back, other than I was working for nine dollars an hour moving boxes of tests taken by kids I used to resemble. I didn't tell my parents that I didn't know if I had made a mistake by not taking over Grandpa Dennis's farm. I didn't say that I couldn't picture my future and that in some ways, it felt like I no longer had a past. Instead, all I had in Iowa City was a present that I wanted to escape.

On a Flat Road

ON AN OVERCAST DAY IN MARCH, with the sun only in the sky to bleach it another shade of gray, I received a phone call from my parents. They said that my grandfather's farm had been sold. He still had to milk until the paperwork was completed, but there was an agreement. I told them that I had to go and then hung up. I'm not a person who cries. At least, that is never my first reaction to anything. I don't look for something to throw and I seldom curse out loud.

Instead, I started walking.

I passed through the length of Iowa City in one direction. I went through the streets I knew and then ones where I had never been. I left the city limits with my hands in my pockets. Soon I was on quiet roads where only an occasional pickup truck passed. There were unplowed cornfields on both sides of me. The stubble of old stalks stuck through the ground, bent in angles between faded tractor tread, and stretched for miles under the washed-out sky. The landscape stood in for what I was feeling, since it took a while to articulate it to myself.

At the time, I was surprised not to be included in the decision, although I shouldn't have been. Farm business was kept guarded. It wasn't something to be discussed at the kitchen table. More than that, though, I had forfeited my share in it. I had worked alongside my family since the age of twelve, and my compensation was to be a part of that work. However, it wasn't until I stopped walking and stared out at the road, which seemed endless because there were no hills, that I realized what I gave up when I came back to Iowa.

Maybe part of me expected to be asked one more time, definitively. However, that's not how things are done in our family. We don't instigate dramatic moments. Instead, we read each other and make assumptions on what we see. Going back to Iowa spoke loudly in place of anything I should have said. Now it was too late. Some big events shake the ground, stopping everyone where they stand. The rubble is there for the whole world to see. Others slip by quietly but still carry devastating impact.

Eventually, I started walking back towards a city for which I had exchanged my inheritance, and which was not my home.

Notes on the American Dairy Industry

THE YEARS 2002, 2003, AND 2006 all returned a yearly average of $12 per hundredweight of milk. The USDA estimated that the cost of producing milk in 2005 was $18 to $19 per hundredweight. When the consequences of the 1996 Farm Bill became clear, the government reversed course and implemented the Milk Income Loss Contract (MILC) in 2002, which once again put a price support floor on milk for the next ten years. However, even under the MILC program, most years the milk checks farmers received were lower than the cost of production. According to Food and Water Watch, the average dairy farm only turned a profit twice between 2000 and 2021.

During the early twenty-first century, the global market was pushed as the liberator of American dairy farming. In 1995, the United States Dairy Export Council was created in order to increase dairy exports. Exports were meant to take care of excess milk production and bring back reasonable returns for farmers. However, the world market proved to be undependable in supporting farm income, instead lowering prices and increasing volatility. Reliance on exports became even more tenuous as the European Union began phasing out milk quotas in 2009. While US farm exports increased by a factor of eight between 2000 and 2020, that was because the portion paid to farmers was kept low and US farmgate prices continued to fall. The largest benefactor of the focus on exporting was agribusiness, which prospered from low milk prices and export incentives.

Traditional economics might have suggested that eventually the milk price would have leveled off as more farmers went out of business. However, as economist Willard Cochrane predicted in the 1950s,

American agriculture found itself on what he called "the productivist treadmill." As the milk price lowered, farms expanded to make up the tighter margins. As more farms became larger, the milk price fell further, encouraging farms to increase their herds again. Between 2002 and 2020, the United States loss an average of 2,300 dairy farms per year, while the national milk supply rose steadily. American agriculture had taken on its new shape: large farms getting bigger and small farms disappearing.

The American Farm Bureau Federation trademarked the slogan "The voice of agriculture" in 2007. However, since its inception almost eight decades earlier, Farm Bureau has consistently sided with large farms and agribusiness to the detriment of family farms on issues including crop subsidies, the concentration of agricultural markets, supply control, and environmental regulation. The organization's scope has grown so large, with a lobbying budget that far outweighs associations working on behalf of family farms, that it is often said that they have the power to singlehandedly kill or pass bills, especially at the level of state legislatures.

The American government, too, quietly took a side on the type of agriculture it wanted. It could have enacted policies to help support family farms, at least enough to fill the gap in the economies of scale they suffered. That would have discouraged further expansion and kept smaller farms sustainable. However, it didn't happen. Agriculture is no longer an issue that gets presidents elected. It has been suggested that when Democrats take office, they find the problem too big to address during their term. When Republicans step in, they insist on allowing the free market to run its course. Regardless of who is in charge, the American government favors cheap food, which is a talking point that does resonate on the ballot. Despite what it costs the people who produce our food, no elected official wants to raise the price of dairy products to consumers. Instead, it has been easier to celebrate the profits that agribusiness makes on the world market as American exceptionalism than to support the family farms the nation was founded on.

In addition to the US government deciding not to back family agriculture, it looked the other way at the sins of factory farms. This ethos was driven in part by the American Farm Bureau Federation and its powerful lobbying influence. Farm Bureau was successful in preventing environmental regulations from being enforced against big dairies, as well as encouraged Washington to privilege the interests of large farms. For example, in 2005 the Environmental Protection Agency granted large farms an exception to the Clean Air Act, a reprieve that was meant to be temporary but has remained in place through successive presidents. This occurred despite the fact that large farms are often responsible for air pollution that harms nearby residents, particularly in Western states, where a valley may be home to numerous factory farms. Farm Bureau has sued the EPA several times since then in an attempt to limit environmental regulations being imposed on agriculture.

At the turn of the century, the family dairy farm was alone and struggling. Farmers in commercials might have had red barns and happy cows on pasture, and that might have been how most Americans thought of dairy farming then, but many of those barns were being boarded up for the last time.

III.
Choices

Haunting

W<small>E STAND OUTSIDE OUR MEMORIES</small> and add our own hues to them. It's difficult to look behind without seeing reflections of the present. Now, as an adult, however, I find myself always looking back. Anything I've gained in figuring out who I'm supposed to be or what I'm supposed to do starts with inhabiting the past.

I walk towards the house and lying in the grass is the Wiffle bat we used to hit walnuts out of the lawn. Sometimes I see the spackled rubber ball that we played with when we were even younger, until it got washed down the creek during a heavy rain. Cattle roam in the pasture next to me and they look good, moving along the sidehill, grazing. To try to get the date right, I look back to the driveway and see what car is there. My father kept farm trucks until there wasn't much left of them, but my mother traded in her vehicles when it made sense.

On the porch there are always boots, split wood, and the propane grill with its handle fallen off. The rescue dog my mother brought home later always took someone's work shoe and left it somewhere in the lawn, making that person curse the next time they came out of the house. Emily, however, who we had most of my childhood and adolescence, didn't do that. Instead, she waited by the door for one of us to wipe her feet and let her in.

Sometimes there's a pink bicycle on the porch. It belonged to my sister when she was small. I don't know if this is true, but I usually imagine it with streamers coming off the handlebars and the word *princess* painted across the frame. I remember the bike because once, on his way to milk, my father rode it. I don't know why, but he started peddling as fast as he could. He was hunched over and his knees stuck out. The deck was three feet high and he went off the end of it without slowing down. He landed squarely, but his momentum took him over the handlebars.

If I look in the kitchen window, I might find my mother. She would be cutting out coupons and putting them in a red fanny pack that she brought to the store. Once they built Aldi's, we started shopping there, but before then, when my sister and I were small, my mother brought us on her biweekly grocery runs and we had to hunt down the box of cereal or dish soap that matched the clippings. Some years, my mother would be at the kitchen table, studying for her master's or preparing for a class she would teach the next day. She had jeans and a T-shirt on, good clothes and barn clothes separated only by how worn they were.

While I am looking in from the porch my mother is looking out the other window, towards the barn. Maybe she is waiting for my father.

My sister could have been anywhere, in class or in the barn forking hay to heifers, but in this timescape, she's at the pond. A boy in the grade above her invited her there. The fact that it actually happened in school matters less than my tendency to remember it being the top of the hill. He gives her a teddy bear and asks if they can date. She doesn't say yes, but she should. Even if they don't stay together for long, it means that someone would have treated her right for a while, and that is something my sister deserved.

Maybe it's fairer, though, to find her riding horses or practicing her heifer to lead. She did the same 4-H activities that I did, and while she was good at all of them, she was best at showing. She won Master Showman at an earlier age than me. Still, that didn't keep me from telling her that I was always better than her. Here, I should tell my sister that one day I will grow up and realize that I should have been nicer to her when we were children.

It's almost a mile from our house to my grandparents' house. Sometimes I dribbled my basketball there, crisscrossing the pavement and pretending to take game-winning shots. From the age of ten, I could drive the Gator and, two years later, the loader tractor, but the Gator was faster. Emily climbs over the passenger seat and rides in the back, spinning in circles as we go down the road. I pull into my grandparents' driveway and kick off my boots on the porch.

I stand in the doorway of the back room and watch my father and grandfather across the kitchen. They're leaning back in their chairs, their stained hands on the table. They're drinking Black Velvet and ginger ale and both are laughing. That tells me something about when this moment is. The faint droning of the TV can be heard from the living room, where my grandmother is watching the news. During the commercials, she might come to the kitchen for a little while and offer my father a cookie. He'll take one the first time he's asked and then wave them off the second time. My father's eyes are red and watery, because that's what happens to them when he laughs. I can't help but stare at my father and how he looks there.

When I go back and see my family in these memories, I try to tell them what's ahead. I want to warn them. If they knew what was going to happen, maybe they could prepare for it.

However, it's then that I realize that I'm not really there. I'm shouting, but no words come out. My hands bang on the glass, but no one turns. The future is already in motion. I would say, "Look, it's coming," but if they saw me and followed my finger, it would only point to an empty sky.

When the Numbers Don't Work

Every morning, my father milked, washed the parlor, and then fed cows. If he went to the house for his own quick breakfast before loading the mixer wagon, he would change from his rubber boots to his work shoes and put on a different pair of jeans. If he didn't, he fed cows in the same clothes he milked in. That's how it was today. Exhaust bellowed up to the rafters when he turned the key on the tractor hooked to the mixer wagon.

My father might have wondered if we were repeating what happened between my grandfather and Clair. Because farming is one repetition laid on top of another, it's tempting to see everything that occurs as a cycle coming back around. He had years to think that it would be us working together, him a better version of his father and me in his image. Instead, what played out had happened two generations ago—a son left the farm.

Because farming gives a person time to think, really think, all perspectives about me being in Iowa would have been unearthed while he milked, washed the parlor, and fed, moving it around from one corner of his mind to the other. In his worst moments, he would have seen me as unserious and still a child, unable to make the commitment at twenty-three that he had made at seventeen. Other times, he would consider how the farming of his youth was different than that in front of me. These things would have made him angry sometimes, and sometimes only sad. The truth, if there was one, would have been lost by the time it had been turned over and over again inside a tractor cab.

My father switched on the radio. Singing along to country songs helped for a while. However, spending most of his day with an FM station, there wasn't much that he hadn't heard many times before and it was hard to stay conscious of the lyrics. He directed the tractor with one hand draped over the steering wheel, staring through the dust on the windshield. Mostly, I think my father missed me. The future version of me was now gone, one that he would have met at the trench each morning or in one of our kitchens to have a drink after a day in the field. The other version was a thousand miles away.

When my father pulled into the trench my grandfather was already standing there. His hands were on his hips, and he watched my father put his tractor into park.

"What do you know today?" my father said, climbing down the steps.

"I'm done milking," my grandfather said. He threw his hands in front of him. Then he looked up from the ground. "You want the cows? Or else I'm sending them in."

By the time I went to Iowa, most of the small farms in our area were gone. The children of farmers were heading to somewhere else on buses all over the country. Many of the friends that I showed with at the county fair became the last generation of their family to milk cows, moving on to other jobs while an empty barn sat outside their parents' kitchen window. Not that knowing that we weren't original made it easier on anyone. Each of us who went away marooned someone else left with the work of ending a farm, and that brings its own burdens, too.

By that morning, my grandfather had already agreed to sell his farm to one of the big operations in the area. The paperwork had not been processed, however, and he was supposed to keep milking until the sale was final.

Grandpa Dennis was a tired man by then. It was difficult for him to carry on after his brain injury, let alone farm. Now that his life's work would not be passed down, he grew more stubborn and self-focused. In addition to half of the land we owned, my grandparents' barn, house, and the house that Kelly had lived in was offered in the deal. My grandmother wanted to live in a log cabin on the pond. My father made a calculation of how much my grandfather needed to pay off his debt and start construction.

The large farm came back and said that the bank authorized a smaller loan than requested. It didn't matter if that was true or not, since it was the type of hedging that could have been anticipated in a large transaction. My father told my grandfather to remove enough houses and fields from the deal to make the counteroffer fair. He could sell them off later, and probably for more. My grandfather, however, did not care to listen and would not allow my father to be a party to the negotiations. It could have been punishment for not producing a proper heir, or maybe he just wanted to be done with the deal as soon as possible. He wasn't a man to be told what to do, anyway. Instead, my grandfather sold it all for the lower price, one that was too low to get out of debt and build a log cabin.

My father had tried to buy the land from my grandfather. It would have been too much for my father to work himself, and he knew that. The loan officer in charge of my father's account had him email a few financial documents. I don't know what papers they were, but they didn't seem to be enough to suggest that either party was expecting the loan to happen. Because my father did not know how to use a computer at the time, I had to send them for him before I left for Iowa. A few days later there was a one-line response: Sorry Derrick, the numbers just don't work.

The sale was pending and expected to be finalized soon. My grandfather, however, did not bother to wait. No one knows how many days or weeks he had been thinking about not milking anymore, because he wouldn't have told anyone. Maybe the idea was new that day.

My father backed up the trailer to the front of my grandfather's barn. He left enough space so the gate could swing out and funnel towards the door. Before he chained the gates together, however, he put his work shoe on the bottom rung and peered into the building.

It took a moment for the cows to settle out of the shadows. My father counted them.

He strained forward, as if that might help him see something different.

He walked around the back of the barn. Maybe the rear gate had opened and the rest of the herd had gotten out. Some of the steel on the barn's walls had rusted through. A few old oil barrels sat in the weeds. My father stepped around a derelict spreader, the paint chipped off, and a pile of rotting tires with bees circling above them.

The back gates of my grandfather's freestall barn were firmly latched. There were no hoofprints behind them, nor cattle standing loose in the field. My father looked back into the freestalls. My grandfather's barn held 150 milking cattle and had been at capacity since he built it. It was expected that my grandfather was selling off the occasional bred heifer to pay bills. However, what remained betrayed how bad things had gotten on my grandfather's farm, and how much he kept everyone out of his business.

There were only thirty-seven cows.

My grandfather never had hobbies. As far as we knew, he wasn't interested in anything outside of agriculture. He was only a farmer. In total, he was a good farmer and usually found new ways to show that. The full extent of the damage caused by chronic traumatic encephalopathy (CTE), which we eventually knew to call it, was just starting to become known then. However, we saw its full harm before us. His entire identity was confined to thirty-seven ragged cows that got loaded onto the trailer and taken to my father's barn. It was a hard type of ending for anyone, but especially my grandfather.

After he hit his head, my grandfather didn't talk or move much differently. He must have put some effort into hiding his mood swings, drinking, and recurrent frustration, because I was told about them later and didn't see them at the time. The only thing that was plain after the accident was that he didn't have it in him to farm. It's difficult to imagine what that was like for him. Of all the things he patched together through the years to make them work another day, the first thing he failed to fix was himself. Maybe it was like seeing the world through the wrong pair of glasses or trying to walk without a sense of balance. He kept on, however, thinking that if he could keep farming until I finished college then I could take over his farm. Then the thing he did with his life would be kept safe by someone else. He would at least have that. But I didn't take over his farm. And a few months later, he quit hiding how difficult it had been. He decided to stop everything at once.

The conditions of the farm sale had already shown that my grandfather no longer had interest in business transactions or their details. He surely wasn't going to consult with M&T Bank about not milking anymore. However, he still had the predatory loan that he had taken out with them a handful of years ago. My grandfather's milk check was collateral that payments were going to be made, and without it the bank was going to find a way to collect. My father had always wanted to separate the mortgage that linked the two farms, but my grandfather refused because it would have limited his credit line, particularly as he began to struggle more. Now, in one day, my grandfather's debts became my parents' problem.

I am not sure who held up the farm sale. In another poor decision, my grandfather allowed the large farm, owned by four brothers, to work the fields being sold before the deal was settled. With access to the land for free, they were not motivated to finalize the contract. The wife of one of the brothers was a lawyer, which may have also given them the confidence to maximize their advantages. However, it may be more likely that it was M&T Bank that delayed the transaction. The land sale would have taken care of the majority of what my grandfather owed.

They could have put my grandfather's loan in deferment while the final signatures were gathered. However, they didn't do that. Instead, they demanded that the money, nearly seven figures, be paid promptly in one sum. To come up with that amount was impossible. Therefore, the bank tried to take my parents' farm instead.

M&T Bank said they were going to foreclose on the mortgage and repossess our land, our farm, and our house. They told us to sell our cattle and equipment immediately or they would do it themselves. Their lawyers were preparing the paperwork. The bank that encouraged my parents to expand a decade ago now wanted to take all that my family had because my grandfather did not milk thirty-seven cows.

I was home that summer. I had returned from Iowa but had not yet gone to Ireland for the master's. I knew what was going on to some extent, because my father told me about it a few times. I probably didn't say anything back. I couldn't have told him that it would be all right, because that would have been an empty thing to say, nor could I have given any advice. All I could have done was work on the farm and be another person there, which was probably what my father needed the most. There's little doubt that he was panicking, but if he showed it in the ways that other people do, like drinking too much or throwing tantrums, only my mother would have seen it. However, I don't think he did. Instead, he became quieter and sometimes tried too hard to pretend everything was fine. From the outside, maybe everything did look fine. But we knew that we were about to lose it all.

I never found out why Bob Brennan didn't turn my father in for giving the $200,000 to my grandfather. Brennan would have known well the types of relationships farmers had with their banks, and maybe he didn't think that what he saw was fair. He would have known about farming, too, and maybe it was even in his family. Because my father had the loan with the Farm Service Agency, he had to report the situation to Brennan. FSA would have gotten most, if not all, of their loan back if M&T forced my parents to sell everything. Instead, however, Brennan told my parents to fight M&T Bank.

It became a game of chicken between my father and M&T. My father threatened to go bankrupt and walk away from the mortgage if they foreclosed. We would lose the farm, but the bank wouldn't be able to recoup its loan.

After the morning milking, I bedded the calves and then found my father. I followed him around until he was ready to feed the cows, and then I climbed into the tractor cab with him. We went down the dug road behind the barn, inside the ruts already there. Goldenrod brushed along the sides of the tires. The John Deere attached to the mixer wagon was older, remaining from when my father milked in the tiestall barn. The brown felt of the ceiling still drooped down and almost grazed the top of my father's head. Whenever I had something on my mind, he knew how to talk about it, drawing it out patiently with considered questions. I didn't know how to do that. The best I could do was to join him in the silence and also yell at Emily when she barked inside the cab.

The creek bed ran beneath the road, and the banks around the bridge were flush with willows, blackcap bushes, and ditchgrass in the dark green foliage of summer. In autumn, the sun would illuminate the dew on their leaves late into the morning, but at this time of year, it had already evaporated. Having passed the creek every day, we knew the phases of the vegetation that came into bloom and then receded back into the season. My father slowed the tractor and looked both ways before merging onto the next road.

We turned into the trench and the mixer wagon behind us rocked back and forth from the driveway's unevenness. A woodchuck shot out of the grain shed, scampering on its short legs.

"That gets me every time," my father said.

I climbed out of the cab first, holding the grab bar as I descended. Then I called Emily, and she jumped over my father's work shoes and waited on the top step for me to lower her to the ground. Finally, my father released his grip on the steering wheel and followed us. On his way to the loader tractor, though, he stopped and turned towards the bunkers again. He said, "There's something about the smell of silage, isn't there?"

One day, looking back at that moment, I realized that the potential of loss is held in every detail.

Fortunately, when Andy Dennis crossed his arms and declared that he didn't pay liens, he was a man of his word. Ironically, the same liens against the property that kept my father from getting a spring planting loan also helped keep M&T from foreclosing. They didn't want to have to pay those liens themselves. Brennan was right: the bank tried to bully my father but in the end didn't dare follow through and lose its investment.

M&T Bank didn't seize the farm, but they also didn't make things any easier for my father. They took their revenge. Each dairy farm receives two milk checks a month: a smaller sum advanced in the first week and a larger check a couple of weeks later. The bank requisitioned the bigger deposit and called it interest. Our farm was already losing money, and now it had to get by on far less. I think we all believed that such circumstances would only last a month or two, and they could have if only the sale of my grandfather's farm was processed. However, it wasn't. Month after month someone, perhaps the bank, refused to submit the paperwork, putting the farm in a hole that it would never get out of.

My father faced down an institution spread across the entire Mid-Atlantic to save our home. Unfortunately, and especially after the rise of agribusiness, farmers maltreated by corporations became increasingly familiar in the history of American agriculture. A logo helps diffuse responsibility. Still, there are individuals in the institutions who make decisions. There was no requirement or precedent to take the majority of a farm's income for as long as M&T did. It appeared that someone decided that the financial gain for the institution was worth the hardship of a single family and had the privilege of hiding behind the letters "Inc." In the same way, I don't know why Bob Brennan stepped outside of his role of FSA agent to help us. My father had already given him enough headaches at his job. Maybe he had already seen too many farmers lose what they had.

My family's account at M&T was handled by a woman named Sandra, but she insisted that she was receiving instructions from higher up. The bank had been Central Trust when my father and grandfather took out their first mortgage, but then it was bought by M&T. Sandra felt bad about the ugliness of M&T's actions, because a year later she called my father and asked if she could visit my grandparents to apologize. Showing up at my grandparents' door was a small act of courage, while validating how malicious the behavior of the bank had been. However, it didn't change the harm it did to our family.

My father went to the trench the morning after my grandfather quit milking. He had to, because he had to feed his cows. When he arrived, no one else was there. He climbed out of his tractor and shut the door on the radio, and then pulled back the plastic on the silage pit, pinning it beneath some old tires. My father reached the loader tractor and found Emily already waiting there. He pushed her up the steps so she could take her place by the steering column. He turned the tractor on, and she barked, and my father yelled at her to be quiet, even though it did no good. Then he followed the tractor ruts to the silage bunker, trying to calculate how much more thirty-seven cows ate.

Stories in an Old Shed

MY FATHER ASKED FOR HELP CLEANING OUT my grandfather's shed. I still had a few months before I was to fly to Ireland for the master's program.

I had come back from school for Christmas and summer throughout my university semesters. However, that last trip to Iowa permanently affixed a pattern, one that would repeat itself indefinitely. In the coming years, I would teach in Germany, get a Fulbright to Iceland, and then return to Ireland for a doctorate. The things I did off the farm, in the places that I went to, had dates to benchmark them. Time on the farm from then on, however, was indeterminant. All I knew was that whenever I came back, it seemed like I was continuing where I left off, though everything was irrevocably different.

For my father, waiting to get the farm's income back, time was painfully concrete. Each day was a measure of burden when it didn't happen. Whatever he thought it would take to recover, he had to recalculate at the beginning of every month. If he wondered if he was starting to fool himself, he didn't tell anyone.

It was just the two of us and we mostly worked in silence, dumping tools into five-gallon buckets and carrying away old compressors and barn fans. My father would look over a PTO shaft or plow coulter, turning it in his hands before throwing it into the back of the trailer to take to the scrap yard. He had worked with my grandfather all his life, sharing the land and machinery, so I knew that he saw things in the dusty objects that I did not. Before the day was over, he mentioned that cleaning out that shed was hard, and that was the kind of thing he seldom said.

At one point, we had to lift an old tractor door together. "You probably don't remember the John Deere this belonged to, do you?" he said.

He then told about a day he disked the Beehive Field as a young teen-ager while my grandfather started planting it. After a few hours, my grandfather eased his tractor to a halt and stopped to piss next to the front tire. My father also pulled his parking brake and, looking to sur-prise him, threw a small flat stone toward his father's feet. The stone curved through the air, hit my grandfather on the back of the head, and dropped him to his knees. As the story goes, my grandfather recollected himself and pulled up his pants. He immediately remarked, "I think I got some on my hands." I had heard that anecdote a few times but always enjoyed listening to my father tell it. Although he never said this to me, I believe that my grandfather taking the moment with humor made my father feel like an adult.

In the end, instead of three generations farming together, my grand-father and I stranded my father. We each distanced ourselves from the farm, and it was now up to my father to handle the consequences. In that way, I emulated my grandfather after all.

My grandfather's shed was large. The planter was always kept in it, with leftover bags of seed piled around the tires, but it usually held other implements at the same time. All the benches were covered in tools, pipe elbows, chains, bearings, washers, and whatever was used to fix something or had broken off from something else. We always had a hard time finding a grease gun when we needed it, but we eventu-ally took out eight from the shed that day. My father had farmed with my grandfather, and these were the things my grandfather farmed with. We hauled them away by the truckload. I had the sense that there was more my father could have said about what we carried, if he had been able. However, the weight of the memories attached to them made them heavier for my father to load.

It was in my father's nature to tell stories. Before, I thought they were entertainment, but eventually I learned that they were his compensa-tion. Most people who farmed long enough saw the milk check fail to cover the costs of feed and fuel, and watched their equipment get older without being able to do anything about it. Still, like everyone else, they had to make sense of what they did and the reasons for it. A narrative is a way to have ownership over what is difficult to hang on to. If you can tell a story about something, then it is not entirely gone. Eventually I began to realize that, whether or not I would ever become a farmer, it was my place to listen to what people like my father said.

Notes on the Gothic

I GOT BOTH HANDS UNDER THE UTERUS TO LIFT IT and levered my elbows against my chest. It spilled over the sides of my palms, feeling like rubber and getting stickier as it dried. After a few seconds my arms started to shake, and my breath strained. The cow had stopped chewing and stared ahead with wide eyes. My father poured diluted teat dip over the organ. It ran down the creases of tissue and into my sleeve.

I had been feeding calves when I heard my name called. I followed the voice until I found my father in the sick pen, standing behind a cow with a prolapsed uterus. She was on her feet, tied to a pole and chewing her cud, but hanging below her tail was a bulbous mass. It was red, but darkening, with button-shaped caruncles all over it.

"Hold on," my father said.

We seldom called the vet anymore. My father had seen enough cows and what ails them to do basic vet work. If a cow had milk fever after calving, my father found the artery in her neck to give her a bottle of calcium. If she had sunken eyes, he put a magnet down her throat, in case she had swallowed a nail or a piece of wire. If she didn't get better, then he tried penicillin, and if that didn't work, he sent her in for beef, as long as he thought she wasn't going to die on the truck. For some things, however, my father had to be more inventive.

After my father poured warm water and iodine over the tissue, he got underneath the uterus himself. He lifted it out of my hands and slowly pushed it back inside the cow. Sometimes she shifted on her hind legs or swung her back end around, but she mostly stood still. Once the uterus was in the right position again my father extended his arm through her vulva. Then he told me to slide my hand against his and take his place.

The decline of a dairy farm is an uncomfortable sight. The farm was a business with little profit under normal circumstances, and my father had to keep it running with only a portion of its cash flow. The scope of his plans was now not seasonal, but day-to-day, trying to get to the next milking. Whatever broke, my father had to fix it with what we had. Money was only found for parts of machines that were needed that day. My father's face sometimes smelled like diesel fuel because he siphoned it from one tractor to put into another. Bills weren't paid until we needed that mechanic or company again. Land taxes came due every year. My father sold the bulldozer to help pay them, and then the John Deere 4320, because we could get by without it.

The twenty-first century continued outside our barn, during which it became apparent that the downturn in dairy farming was not cyclical, but its new reality. Low prices further pushed the change in the industry. With tight margins, the economies of scale became increasingly necessary, and more farms were driven into Butz's mandate of getting big or going out. The number of cows needed to break even was more than what we, and most of our neighbors, had in our freestalls. Family farms disappeared outside of small towns in a way never seen before. Those that were left found themselves competing against large operations that had lower costs. Not long into the new millennium, it became clear that it was no longer the farmer against the world as we had always thought, but the small farmer versus the large farmer.

For our family, the differences in farming were not abstract but something we drove by every day. As soon as my grandfather's farm was sold, the operation that bought it hired a bulldozer. They removed the diversion ditches and hedgerows that had been part of the fields for generations. It gave them a few more acres to plant. Immediately, however, topsoil was lost in runoff. We eventually noticed fewer types of birds in the area. Some fields, out of view, were only used to dump manure. The families of small farms live on the land they work and have a stake in managing it well. Calling it a home means something, and not just for the farmer. Small townships like Canaseraga survived with family farms because money and people stayed in them, and they were more than a hinterland to spread manure on. It also matters to the cows, as well as the environment. When a cow is on pasture it adds less ammonia and greenhouse gas to the atmosphere. Our herd had access to pasture from spring to autumn. Cows on large farms never see sunlight. Big farms produce milk more cheaply, but there are greater costs that come due later. Because of that, there has always been a case for smaller agriculture. It just hasn't been made very loudly.

⌒

Whatever complaints my father had about the state of the dairy industry, he had already offered them during morning milkings. For now, he worked quietly, taking a steak knife out of his back pocket. I didn't see it until then and realized that he must have gone to the house and snuck it out of the kitchen drawer. He slowly began twisting holes in the vulva around my arm. He asked me how I was doing, and I said okay. He worked on one side of me, and then the next.

My mother didn't get to use any of her paychecks. She was teaching animal science at a high school and listening to her colleagues talk about the trips they took or the remodeling they were doing on their bathrooms. Instead, what was left of her salary that didn't go to a car payment or heating the house was put towards something the farm needed at that moment. She was already used to having less because she married into a farm, but this was a big sacrifice to make month after month.

When my father was done, he slipped the knife into his back pocket and told me not to tell my mother that we had used it. Then he bent down and pulled out one of his shoelaces. It stretched to the length of his waist before it finally came free. He tossed it into the bucket that had held the iodine and swirled it around in what was left. Then he picked it out and began threading it through the holes he had made.

The farm started to look rougher. There wasn't the time, and maybe the will, to do things like pick up piles of netwrap, paint the calf hutches, or nail down steel sheets that had lifted off the barn's roof. That was beyond the remit of surviving, and surviving took what we had. However, we might have just imagined that there were more cobwebs in the corners or metal rusting on machines because that was how farming felt. Watching the cows get thinner, the milk weights lower, and equipment become more ramshackle was hard. It seemed like bad farming, and that wasn't the kind of farmers we were. My father kept going, though, trying to hide his stress. Often while he worked, he would say to himself, "Come on, man, rock 'n' roll this shit." All day, he passed between feeding something, milking something, or doing some sort of fieldwork, and whoever was around and listened would eventually hear Rick Dennis tell himself to rock 'n' roll. That helped keep us from panicking. However, the grim details around us reflected what we were thinking.

Eventually the shoelace went the circumference of the vulva. My father had me remove my hand before he tied the two ends together into a bow. Then we washed our arms in the milk house sink and headed towards the porch, my father walking gingerly to keep his work shoe on his foot.

What We Reach For

On September 11, 2008, I read an email from my sister. It was the same day, seven years earlier, that my grandfather had hit his head in the milking parlor. I set my coffee next to my laptop. The classes for my master's program started in Galway that week. The subject of the message said "VERY IMPORTANT FROM HOME!!!"

There had been no rain the day before in Canaseraga. My father was probably planning to chop corn. Because he had to do it by himself, he had to fill a wagon, unhook it from the chopper, connect it to the Ford tractor, dump it, and then switch it back onto the chopper. It was slow progress for one man alone. That probably made the days feel long. However, the leaves had started to change color in the valley by then. There would be a nice view from the tractor window.

That morning milking was probably no different than any other. Something would have to happen to make it stand out from all the years of putting milkers on and taking them off. It was another daybreak of sliding on the barn boots, getting the cows from the stalls, and preparing their udders to be milked. It was the same motion as always: dipping the teats, wiping them, and then attaching the milkers. It nearly happened on its own, the hands carrying it out and leaving the mind to itself. My father had a lot to think about. He had to figure out how to get the sale of my grandfather's farm processed so he could get his milk check back. He had to find a way to pay for the bills on our kitchen table.

The weather being good, the cows were still on pasture. Once each group had been milked, they would have trotted through the freestall alleys and back outside. Sometimes they kicked their hind legs in the air when they left the barn, happy all over again to find the gate still open.

Because they were outside most of the time, the barn didn't need to get scraped as often. However, it had to be scraped that day.

My father had the arms of the skid steer raised to put new pins in their joints. Box-shaped and smaller than tractors, skid steers seem relatively harmless, except being easy to tip over if lifting something too heavy. We used it mainly for scraping the manure in the narrow alleys of the free-stall barns. Its metal cage with the large safety bar in front gives a sense of security. The worst that could usually happen with a skid steer is to back into a gate or mishandle the levers and slam the bucket on the concrete.

A series of gates directed cattle in the freestall barn. Scraping out the alleyways, my father had to get out of the skid steer, open a gate, get back in to drive to the next gate, and then get out again. The skid steer has a kill switch that turns off the machine every time the driver gets out of the seat. It's a safety precaution. However, it also means restarting the skid steer over and over again while scraping. My father did what he shouldn't have done, and what many farmers are guilty of: he disabled the switch.

My father raised the arms of the skid steer and then crawled out underneath them. The large metal bucket hung over his head. He looked behind the seat, moving around a grease gun and an operator's manual until he found the mallet. The skid steer was old enough that the pins had worn down, so he had bought replacements. Meanwhile, the machine hummed quietly, rocking on its tires.

My father stood underneath the metallic arms that were half-rusted and mostly covered in manure. He moved back and forth to find the right angle to tap the pin through the joint. At some point, the end of his shirt fell over one of the levers. My father went to move away from the cab, but the fabric pulled on the handle and brought the arms down on top of him, crushing him against the skid steer.

The force of the machine broke his vertebrae, shattered his ribs, and tore apart the right side of his diaphragm. The metal continued to push into his body. It couldn't flex much more without disintegrating. He lifted his arm towards the lever, but he couldn't reach it.

He was going to die.

Most boys think that their fathers can fix anything. There's always the chance that maybe they're invincible after all. One day I realized that feeling had never really left me. Part of it, I think, was that I couldn't fix much or solve any problems in front of me, not like he could. He was capable by nature. But I also think that maybe there was something more in my dad that wasn't in other fathers. For all the movies where things look helpless for the hero until the background score picks up and with one final brave act he saves himself, I don't think any music played for my father. I don't know if his life flashed before him, or if he imagined my mother finding him there like that, or thought of us living without him. Maybe it was just pain. Either way, my father was in the process of accepting death, but then decided not to.

My father stretched for the lever again. It was just out of his grasp. He leaned as much as he could, reaching towards it for the next twenty minutes. He pressed himself forward, the machine tightening on him a little more every millimeter he gained, tearing him apart. It was unlikely that his bones had the distance left in them. As natural as it is for the mind and body to separate themselves during the routine of farmwork, this time his mind had to stay with his body. At least long enough to give my father a chance to reach the lever.

Somehow, his fingers made it to the handle and pulled it. He fell to the concrete, broken.

My father lay on the floor of the barn for hours. He might have cried, but then again, there might not have been enough left of him to cry. If he could have found breath inside him, he could have yelled for help, but it wouldn't have been heard over the sound of the engine. The only person around was my mother, and she was in the house. All the other farmers had cell phones by then, even if just to allay their spouses' fears against moments like this. Our farm, however, was in a dip in the valley, a geography that kept us from getting reception. My father couldn't call for help. He couldn't say goodbye to anyone or tell them that he loved them. Instead, all he could do was curl up on the concrete, preparing to disappear while smoke from the skid steer's exhaust hung above him.

The day the dry cow pinned my father into the corner of the feeder wagon was the only time I saw him react to pain. It was shocking, because it had never occurred to me that something could be more than my father could handle. His ability to continue on, no matter how bad everything got, was what kept all of us going. He was a strong man. I don't know where it came from or how it was possible, but there was still an ember of toughness in my father that wasn't used up yet. He decided once again to try to live.

My father couldn't move anything below his shoulders. All he could do was drag himself forward on his elbows one inch at a time. Inside his skin some of his bones hung at odd angles. He let out a sound every time he heaved, carrying the damage with him. His elbows were wet with the cold manure seeping through the fabric, and eventually they bled. Still, he pulled himself towards the parlor. It would have been quicker to go to the end of the alley, but there was a gate there. It was too low to crawl under, and he could not raise himself to unlatch it. His body left a wide, shallow furrow as he dragged himself through the manure, making jagged edges every time he lurched.

He got to the holding area and then to the parlor. The parlor's cement was still wet from being hosed down after the morning milking. The wall next to him was stained yellow and brown from all the cows that passed through it. The corners of the ceiling had cobwebs in them because no one usually looked up to spray the hose there. His fingers gripped the manure grates to pull forward. The weight of his legs and abdomen rasped along the floor. In the end, he had returned to the place where he went every morning and most evenings since it was built, where the act of carrying on for another day always started. It was there, in the parlor, that he had exhausted every bit of fight in him and finally waited to die.

The Waiting

THE PRINCIPAL CAUGHT MY MOTHER as she was heading out the school door. She asked if my mother would mind correcting papers for a teacher who was out. The students could use the feedback, the principal said. My mother had only started working there a few years earlier and was not tenured. Her response would have been different had she known at the time that they did not plan to give her tenure. As it were, she forced a smile and took the armload of lab write-ups.

Back home, my mother sat at the kitchen table with the stack of papers. Usually, she went out to help my father milk while they talked about their day, but first she had to finish grading. My father hadn't come in for a cup of coffee before milking, nor had she seen him cross the driveway from the barn to the shed. She figured he had probably gone straight from the field to the parlor, since trying to both chop corn and milk kept him busy.

My mother grew up over the hill, less than a mile away. From the age of four she spent most of her summers at her grandparents' farm around the corner. Later, she went to Virginia Tech for animal science and had ideas about becoming a vet or getting a PhD. While in college she started dating my father. In a faded *County Living* article, she tells about selling her cow that she raised on her grandparents' farm and having to marry the farmer to get it back. My parents wed soon after she graduated from Virginia Tech.

Above where my mother worked at the kitchen table, among pictures of the family, was a framed diploma from the University of London. At that point in her life, my mother had never been abroad. I was born a few years after my parents got married, and my sister three years later. While raising us, she also worked on the farm but didn't have much opportunity to start a career of her own. When my sister and I could take care of ourselves, my mother earned a master's degree from the University of London through correspondence courses. She sent her assignments in by mail and got the feedback in the post weeks later. Then she became a teacher. It was important for her to have her own occupation. It was also necessary for the family to have extra income and access to health care.

My mother had almost finished the papers in front of her. She looked forward to getting out of the house. It had been a long day, and she wanted to complain about the principal to my father. However, as she neared the last assignments a nagging thought settled over her: she couldn't hear the vacuum pump. The pump would be on if my father was milking, and he hadn't left because his pickup was in the driveway. Similar worry had come to nothing before, but still, she put on her clothes and hurried to the milking parlor.

My sister sat at her computer in her apartment, doing her homework. Her classes were done for the day. She was in her first semester at SUNY Geneseo, studying to be a biology teacher like my mother.

When I left for college, my sister stepped into a lot of the same work that I used to do on the farm. She, too, had been encouraged by our parents to get a degree to ensure that she would have opportunities, but she had always assumed that she would be involved in agriculture. As far as I knew, she was never considered to take over my grandfather's farm. She was likely too young at the time, and perhaps the notion of a female running an operation was an idea my grandfather was not familiar with. Still, she thought that if she did not have her own farm, she could at least have a bigger part in the one she grew up on. Until then, she had to prove that she was as capable as anyone else, so she milked, baled hay, and planted corn like any other dairy farmer.

While at her desk, she received a message on AOL Instant Messenger from a friend in Canaseraga. He asked if her father was okay. This friend had an ambulance scanner, and it came across it that Rick Dennis had been hurt by a skidder. My sister told her friend that we didn't do any logging and didn't have a skidder.

My sister called the home phone. Grandma Kramer picked up after one ring, shouted "Hello" frantically, and then hung up.

My sister got in her car.

Geneseo is forty-five minutes away from Canaseraga. Halfway there, my sister's cell phone rang. It took away any hope that there was a misunderstanding or that the accident wasn't so serious. My mother told her to go to the Canaseraga Firehall, because that was where they were airlifting my father to Strong Memorial Hospital in Rochester. My sister drove faster, her tears blurring the road.

The helicopter was already gone by the time my sister barreled into the driveway of the firehall and slammed on the brakes. My mother was still there, however, waiting for her so they could go to Rochester together. Grandma Kramer drove them up, now that she didn't have to stand by the phone in case the ambulance called, even if that was unlikely. My mother said over and over how pale my father looked and that she was worried he wasn't going to make it.

My sister wasn't the only person to hear about the accident as soon as my father was discovered. Word spread fast among the community that Rick Dennis had been badly hurt. Over fifty people arrived at the farm with the Canaseraga emergency crew. My father had lain in the parlor for five hours until my mother had found him, but now everyone pitched in to get him out of there as quickly as possible. They couldn't back up the ambulance to the closest end of the barn because one of the tractors was in the way. Instead, they carried my father through the barn on the stretcher, one person handing him over to someone else, who then passed him along. Being a farmer, my father was seldom in town, except to get a part from the tractor dealership or to watch a girls' basketball game. He probably didn't know how well he was regarded.

At the firehall, my father was loaded into the helicopter. He was barely conscious. The manure in his clothes rubbed into the stretcher beneath him. Someone had taken off his boots, and his socks were stained and mismatched. He tried to form a few words, but the emergency crew told him to relax. In addition to my mother and grandmother, some of the people at the farm followed the ambulance there. Everyone stood in the driveway of the firehall as the helicopter's propellers started to move. Because it happened rarely, many in Canaseraga would have stopped what they were doing and looked up. If they did, they would have seen my father lifted into the sky and taken away.

The operation was scheduled for the next morning. Jane, the hired hand, had agreed to take the morning milking so that both my mother and sister could go to Rochester for my father's surgery. However, that morning Jane knocked on the door of the house and started coughing. She said she was too sick to work. As a result, my sister had to stay behind to milk while my mother went to the hospital.

By now, my sister had milked alone many times. The rhythms of how it was done were stored in her body. However, none of those mornings were like this. It was only the memory of the act in her hands that was getting it done this time. She tried to hold it together long enough to finish the milking, so she could go to the house and make a phone call to see if her father was still alive.

She was down to the last cows when the shorthorn heifer came in. She was my sister's cow and had freshened a week ago. The hired hand had tied her back legs the first time she went into the parlor, and since then she wouldn't tolerate the milker being on her. She kicked my sister as my sister tried to hold the milker in place and get through the end of the milking. The shorthorn kept striking her arm, however, covering it in manure and red marks. That's when my sister lost it.

Tom Capwell walked into the parlor to find my sister crying. The Capwells had a dairy farm in Canaseraga and when they stopped milking cows they bought the small grocery store in town. Tom came to see if there was anything he could do to help. When he saw my sister he stepped into the pit, took the milker dangling over the pipe, and put it on the shorthorn. He held onto the milker while the shorthorn kicked him over and over again. There was one more group to go. Tom and my sister milked in silence, my sister rubbing her manure-covered arms on her cheeks. When they were done, she went to the house and called the hospital.

Learning It All Over Again

Wʜᴇɴ ᴍʏ ꜰᴀᴛʜᴇʀ ᴀʀʀɪᴠᴇᴅ at Strong Memorial Hospital, he was placed on a steel gurney in the ER among others who were sick or injured. The first doctor leaned over him, putting a flashlight in his eyes and pressing where his organs were.

"He's going to die," he said. "It's not right to waste a surgery on him." The doctor handed the clipboard back to the nurse and walked down the hallway.

A second and then third surgeon were sought. They, too, did not believe it to be worth the effort.

There was a younger doctor who found out about my father's case. He was Italian American and confident. Maybe he was also compassionate. He had performed a similar surgery once before, and that person never walked. In addition to putting a metal rod in my father's back and fusing the vertebrae, he had to rebuild the abdominal wall on my father's right side. It was nearly an impossible task, which might have been the attraction for him. The doctor didn't have anything to lose. My father was supposed to die anyway.

My mother called my father's parents and told them where they could find the ER.

My grandfather wasn't going to go to Rochester. "I'll see him when he gets out," he said.

"You know he might not make it?" my mother said.

A man my mother and sister did not know stood at the entrance of the door and scanned the room. When he saw my father, he came over to him.

At the time of my father's accident, the land sale had not been processed for eight months. My mother's income couldn't feed both the family and the cows for that long, and each day the farm took on debt. More and more repairs had to be done without, until it felt like most things were held together with duct tape or wishful thinking. Whether by coincidence, someone's guilt, or the bank's fear my father could die and they wouldn't get the mortgage back, the paperwork was completed immediately after my father was airlifted to Strong Memorial. It just needed my father's signature.

The man standing next to the gurney was a paralegal. My father was on a lot of morphine and had been told that he probably wasn't going to live. It was not legal to have my father sign a document in that state. However, if my father did survive, our farm needed to start receiving milk checks again, especially since he would not be there for a long time. That would have been the logic, anyway, if my father was coherent enough to follow it. More likely, however, was that my father had a hard time knowing what was going on. The paralegal put the document on my father's chest and my father scribbled a barely legible version of his name.

Aunt Kelly must have convinced my grandfather to go to the hospital, because she arrived with my grandparents before the surgery. They followed gingerly behind her as they weaved through people lying on gurneys who were not their son, other families surrounding them with pale faces.

My mother saw them and nodded. She instinctively took a step back.

My aunt put her hand on my father's forearm. It was a part of him that still looked strong and unbroken, a place she could anchor herself to. "How are you doing?" she asked, her voice breaking high. She started welling up. My grandmother rubbed her back in small circles.

My grandfather stood at the foot of the gurney with his fingers clasped in front of him. His shoulders hunched forward. He looked around him and then tried to gaze off into the distance, but the horizon was behind the white walls of the room.

The light from the fluorescent bulbs overhead fell on my father's gown and the sallow skin beneath it. In the glare, it seemed like he was already fading away. His eyes had trouble following a person for long, and with the morphine he drifted inside himself. He did, however, lift his head off the pillow. "Dad?"

My grandfather hesitated, and then drifted a few steps around the bed to be at my father's side. My grandfather tapped him on the elbow.

"You'll be fine in a few weeks, won't you?" he said. "You don't really need to be here, do you?" He shifted from one foot to another, still gripping his own hands.

Part of my grandfather saw Clair lying in that bed. He knew how that story went, and he couldn't accept it. To him, to be in a hospital meant that you were bound to die. It was the same for the farmer as it was for the cow: if you can't stand up, then you are already dead.

There might have been things that my grandfather wanted to say. However, he stood over my father, broken in his own respect.

Eventually, enough of my father pooled together to utter a few words. "I'll be okay," he said.

My grandfather took a step backwards, towards the door. "He needs to rest," he told my aunt. "We should go."

My grandmother and my aunt lingered around my father. They told him to be strong and that they loved him, and that he was going to come through everything all right. He was a tough man, after all. Then they kissed his head and cried into their hands as they joined my grandfather in the hallway.

My father spent most of the night on the gurney before being moved to a bed in the early morning. A priest came during the evening to read him his last rites, but my father sent him away. A few hours later the surgeon opened the curtains while putting his gloves on. "He's getting stiffer by the minute," he said to the nurses behind him. "Let's give it a go."

Because my sister had to milk, my mother waited alone. How long she sat in the padded chairs or the details of what she did blended into the white halls around her. All she knew was that she was waiting. Pastors from both Protestant churches in Canaseraga visited during this time. One of them offered to milk, since he had done it before on another farm. Although my mother declined, it was a kindness she appreciated.

Years later I asked my mother what she was thinking during those hours in the waiting room. She couldn't tell me. "PTSD, you know," she said. Maybe it's better that way. Starting from our childhoods, the intimacy of our parents is hidden behind closed doors. Any assumption I would make would come from narratives I've read or seen on TV, whether I knew it or not. Instead, they had their own story, and it doesn't belong to me. They were as close as any other couple I've ever seen, and now she was scared. These are facts enough. I can picture her that day, leaning forward on her knees, her head down.

Two hours later, my father woke from the surgery.

The nurses might have had to tolerate the young doctor's boasting. He probably told his colleagues about it. He had saved a life that was thought to be over, which must be one of the highest achievements in the medical field.

Gloat as he might, he then had the task of tempering everyone's expectations. He explained that there was a one-in-a-million chance that my father would ever walk again. His body was broken, having lived through what was unlikely to be survived, and he would be in pain for the rest of his life. He would have to get used to a wheelchair and would always need assistance but should remember to be grateful to be alive and still around his family and friends. In truth, no one knows anymore the exact speech he gave my parents. However, my father nodded, listening politely.

"I'll walk again," my father said. "I decided to."

It was fortunate that my mother's job had good insurance and that my father was on that plan. He had spent most of his life uninsured, and the medical coverage my mother got from her employers before and after the accident was never as comprehensive. When he was admitted, the hospital checked my father's records to see if he would go to the second floor or the fourth floor, the level of care being much better upstairs. The difference, in the end, was likely between life and death.

None of us imagined that our farm could run without my father. There was a lot of work to pick up. However, the hired hand did most of the morning and the night milkings for the first few days, and then Bill Wellington, who had gone to school with Uncle David, took over the morning milking. Uncle David fed the cows and worked out a deal with another farmer to chop our corn for the use of the equipment. Doug Hubbard, one of my father's closest friends from high school, came up every other day to scrape the barn, while Grandpa and Grandma Kramer fed the calves each morning and evening. Knowing that all these people were giving up their time to keep the farm going was what gave my father the motivation to return to it.

The first thing my father learned to do was to put on his socks. He was given a grabbing stick like those used to pick up trash. A nurse would leave his socks on the edge of the bed, and he would try to get the top of one of them with the pinchers and slowly work it over his foot at the other end of his body. It had taken him over two hours the first time he accomplished it.

A week later, my father tried to walk to the end of the hall. After the surgery they began to wean him off the morphine, and then the pain started setting in. All motion hurt, but he kept moving. Sometimes one of the nurses caught him practicing without the occupational therapist. He would be scolded and forced back into bed. He had my mother buy books on identifying birds, even though he had had no interest in them before, and he looked through the pictures until he could try to lift himself out of the sheets again. He became friends with his room-mate, who suffered from terminal cancer. They talked about their lives. Having been close to death, my father felt for a man who wasn't going to escape it.

Meanwhile, the cows continued to get milked and fed because people cared about my father. Even with all the help, though, there was one notable absence.

Skype was around in 2008, but not yet ubiquitous enough that I knew about it, nor any other way to make phone calls through the inter-net. I was given the number of the landline phone in my father's hospi-tal room and allowed to call him a few days after the accident. I had to go to an internet call center in Galway and enter a booth with Plexiglas dividers. My father's voice sounded thin and distant, as if it bore the thousands of miles between us. He said that he was fine and that he had a long road ahead of him, but he was going to make it.

I had called my mother after receiving that frantic email from my sister. She had the defiance of one dealing with tragedy and rising to its level. Everything is under control here, she repeated. I asked if I should come home to help with the farm. She told me: "No. Do not come home. You need to finish your studies, and it would make your father very disappointed if he knew you interrupted your master's program to come back."

That was another defining moment, but I didn't recognize it then. The master's program seemed flexible. I probably could have deferred the semester or the year, or even kept up with the exercises remotely for a month. My mother might not have realized that. Maybe she thought it was harder to travel from another continent than it was, that once someone was across the ocean, they more or less had to stay there. By now, I've had years to return to this telephone call and consider it. I know she was trying to do the right thing, to either relieve me of the obligation or allow it to be my own decision. Nonetheless, the word *disappointed* hung very heavy over me. I didn't like upsetting people, and I still remembered my high school graduation speech.

I should have been old enough to think for myself, independent of my parents. However, I failed that maturity test, too. I didn't know what I should have known: that being an adult not only requires you to make choices but also to realize that there are choices in front of you. Not going back home came from trying to be an obedient son, not out of selfishness. Still, my reasons meant less than the action itself, and remaining in Galway spoke louder than I realized at the time.

When I think about September 2008, I usually feel guilty, but sometimes I get angry. Putting the situation in context, I sometimes think that my mother was trying to take everything on herself, full of determination and adrenaline. If that was the case, she would have had my father as an example. He always went to extremes to avoid asking something from the rest of us. He, too, explicitly said that I should stay in Galway and keep studying. That was why I was shocked when, a few years later, we were having a mild argument and he shouted out: "But you didn't come back when I was hurt."

Maybe, at the time, he really thought that I shouldn't return home after the accident, but seeing everyone else helping out on the farm slowly worked his mind back. Maybe someone said something—look at how much everyone is sacrificing of their own time when his own son couldn't be bothered. Maybe it was on some of their faces, or maybe my father assumed it himself and was embarrassed. Sometimes I wonder if my own mind betrays me and someone did ask me to come back, and I don't remember it.

Regardless, I stayed in Galway and every Sunday went to the call center. Because he didn't have much news to share, he quietly listened to how my day had been. I told him how classes were going, what festivals were on, and how much it rained. Eventually, it felt like part of my identity: the son who did not come back. Whether it was only in my head or not, my character had, in part, been decided. And the worst thing was that once again that crossroads had slipped by without me noticing it.

After two weeks in the hospital, my father went home. I don't know what sort of welcome they had ready for him, or if those helping on the farm simply stopped by the house when they were done in the barn. I knew it made my father anxious to sit indoors while other people were working. When I was growing up, he never let me go to the barn to start the milking or chores without him. After coming home again, he would delicately put on his boots and slowly track the fifty yards from the house to the barn, pushing the walker through the snow. Uncle David would be waiting in the milk house to send him back. He had to be stern with my father. He said, "We're not doing all this just so you can get hurt again."

My father got an infection in his back at the operation site. The surgeon said that he would have to return to Rochester a few more times to have it cleaned and dressed. As the doctor was about to ask the nurse to make an appointment, however, he had an epiphany.

"You work with animals. You can probably treat this yourself."

My mother was given a scalpel and disinfectant. Every few days she cut open my father's back. It left a divot near his vertebrae, but it eventually healed. Before that happened, though, she ran out of bandages.

At the next appointment, the doctor lifted my father's shirt and started nodding.

"Good idea. Maxipads are sterile."

My mother wouldn't allow my sister to defer the semester at Geneseo, so she came back to help with chores between classes, and again at nights and weekends. Most of her professors were understanding, except one who taught animal physiology, who gave her a C. The ability to do farmwork independently was no longer a novelty, but necessary to keep the farm going.

Like the rest of my mother's family, my sister rode horses. Geneseo had a reputable equestrian team, and my sister had been chosen for it just before my father's accident. Somehow she managed to stay on the team after my father got hurt, getting to the stable enough to keep her spot. In November, she had a riding competition. My mother helped my father into the passenger side of the Pontiac sedan. It was the first time he left the hill since the accident. Seeing him there with his walker was one of the most important moments in my sister's life.

There wasn't enough tissue left on my father's right side to keep his organs in place, so they jutted out under his skin. In April he needed another operation to place a wire mesh inside him. It was also a surgery without any guarantees. In fact, because my father opted to have it done at the local hospital, the surgeon there had to read a book to figure out how to do it. The doctor warned that my father needed to be careful, because a second operation was not possible if the first one didn't hold. My father was to avoid any physical activity that was strenuous, lest it tore out his side again. The doctor said that he would fill out the paperwork so that my father could go on disability, but my father politely declined. Perplexed, the doctor instead gave him a lifetime prescription for tramadol.

The mesh held for about two weeks, after which the bulge returned. My father said he could feel the screws loosen inside him. There was nothing he could do about it, so he started milking again. In the end, the man who wasn't supposed to have made it instead found a way to live. Then the man who was supposed to be paralyzed learned to walk again. And then, after all of that, that same man went back to farming.

My father moved slower after the accident. Often his weight shifted from side to side as he walked. When he got tired, his chest tipped forward and he tended to stoop. He got incredibly sore, which was a condition that doctors said would only get worse. Still, he noticed how addictive the painkillers were, years before the opioid crisis came to light, and he weaned himself off them. He kept moving, however, because that was how he knew he was alive.

☞

I went back home in April to run the farm for a few months after my father's second operation. He and my mother met me at the airport.

He wore his gray Syracuse Orangemen hat and an unbuttoned collared shirt, blue and checkered, over a T-shirt. He had a few more gray hairs than I remembered, but his face somehow looked younger in that moment. His eyes were uncommonly blue. I wondered how I had missed how blue his eyes were.

He leaned on a cane, arched forward from the waist. He stood at a different angle from the world now.

If I hesitated, that's because of what important moments do to me. Instead, he immediately grabbed my hand and pulled me in for a hug. It was hard to keep my balance in his grasp. He held on for a long time.

"You're not used to seeing your old man so bent over, are you?"

I was the only person not to have seen his body after the accident, and it might have weighed on his mind. When we walked to the airport parking lot he dabbed at the corners of his eyes.

The old familiarity of seeing our land again still hit me through the tiredness and jetlag. Some fields stood fallow, waiting to be plowed, while young grass grew in others. The hill line and hedgerows still shaped the horizon, and the bends in the road were the same as they were before. However, there was also something else: the sense that the land had moved on, and that things happened on it without me. It was a hard feeling to pin down or make sense of.

I checked the faces of the other family members and people from the community whom I ran into in the coming weeks. I never detected any blame for my not coming back, but it also could have been the sort of thing I was oblivious to. Even the kindest person could be forgiven for having it cross their mind that so many people helped Rick Dennis in his moment of need, when his own son gave nothing.

I went to the milking parlor the first morning I was back. Bill Wellington was there, carrying on with the morning milking as he had done for months. He was about my father's age, quiet and unmarried. He was a hard worker and always found employment somewhere, milking for farmers in the area, collecting blueberries, or working in local factories. He picked up the dipper and wetted the teats with iodine, and I followed after him and wiped them. We made small talk, but not much. The pulsation of the milkers beat on, feeling like it was the whole parlor and not just the inflations that squeezed and released over and over again. Suddenly Bill turned towards me.

"I know what I'm doing," he said.

I didn't realize that Bill could have misinterpreted my presence in the parlor. I hadn't meant to be the owner's son who came back from abroad to see how the help was managing his affairs. I had no right to claim that authority even if I wanted to. Instead, I was there for myself. I had milked thousands of times before that day, but there are always small details that would have changed. The vacuum pump might have needed jerry-rigging, and certain cows required special attention. More than that, though, it was to find my place back in those boots. Whenever I returned home, it usually felt like I slipped into a prior version of myself there and fell into the same rhythms. Still, the transition was never immediate, and it might take a day or two to step in line. This time it took even longer. I told Bill: I don't know what I'm doing.

Ti-Ti

My father passed by with the dipper, and in spite of himself, scratched the back of the cat's neck. The cat lifted his head and looked up to him. He followed the trajectory of my father's hand with blank eyes as my father grabbed paper towels out of his back pocket and started wiping an udder.

"That's one messed-up cat," he said.

The dump trucks echoed in the valley when they shifted gears. Through the screen in the back of the holding area, we saw them race down the hill. In mere days, the large farm took the silage off the fields my grandfather had sold. It wasn't the event that it was with the custom choppers, maybe because we didn't own the land anymore and we weren't part of it. Maybe from the distance of our milking parlor it was clearer that big machines never belonged on those fields to start with. A green mist lifted from the top of the beds as they flew by our house, the forage settling along the shoulder wherever there was a pothole in the road. We had to keep the dog locked in and couldn't ride horses when their trucks went by.

My father's body swayed left and right as he walked the length of the parlor. He wore large, loose shirts that partly merged his bulge into the rest of his shape. He never said he was in pain, but he sighed every time he sat down, and the look on his face when no one was watching said that he was pulling himself through the day. Much of the time I was gone, living in Europe and calling home once a week. Wherever I was, I usually came back a few times a year, often for a month or two. The first few days in the parlor I shared what new anecdotes I could, but after that the two lives I had didn't overlap. When I was back, my mind tried to make me think that I had been on the farm the whole time.

Weeks before, Ti-Ti had stumbled into the parlor as a small, snotty kitten. He stopped at the edge of the pit to tuck his feet under him, curl his tail around his body, and sneeze. I waited for my father to take the hose to him. Cats were not allowed in the milking parlor for general biosecurity reasons. Sometimes, near the end of the milking, they strutted back and forth in front of the doorway with their tails up, aware that they might soon be fed the milk of a treated cow. Still, they knew better than to cross the threshold onto the concrete floor. This sickly kitten, however, showed no regard for the natural order of things.

My father never picked up the hose.

The name Ti-Ti was probably a degeneration of the sound *kitty-kitty*, or maybe it came from some other quick reasoning that leads to barn cats being called what they are. Ti-Ti was an outcast among the other cats and was seldom let near the milk dish. His small frame trembled as he walked up and down the grates between dirty hooves. Once in a while my father grabbed Ti-Ti when he tiptoed by, stroking his coat and then placing him back on the concrete. Sometimes Ti-Ti was stepped on and would let out a howl, but instead of running out of the parlor he walked to the end of the pit, folded his legs, and pinned his ears back. His feet were always wet and matted because, unlike other cats, he was not bothered by treading through manure. He didn't show any reaction to a piece of straw dragged across his paws, nor any other poking or rough play. His face carried on it a dull expression that, if he were a human, could suggest an absence of thought. Once, I caught my father pulling dry dog food out of his pocket and placing it next to Ti-Ti.

"What?" he said without being asked. "He's not going to make it anyway."

It was true that the numbers weren't in Ti-Ti's favor. Even wary, resourceful cats often didn't survive on the farm. Every so often a disease ran through and wiped out most of them, leaving only a small group of the hardiest and luckiest to start breeding again. A few times, in unsightly circumstances, a visitor's vehicle leaked antifreeze into the same puddle that milk was spilt during pickup. I had never seen it myself but was told about how handfuls of cats flopped around the driveway in heinous spasms.

"Yes, he's getting soft," I told my mother, when we teased my father about his affection. However, we never believed that was the reason my father hoped the cat would live. In this case it wasn't pity that led a fifty-year-old man to squirt penicillin in a sickly kitten's eyes. It had more to do with respect. They were meant to be kindred spirits.

Ti-Ti was often kicked by the cows in the parlor and more times than not his coat was tangled with burdocks, but he survived. He usually sat on top of the metal steps, staring into space for no apparent reason. Sometimes, when I put the milkers on each cow in line I stopped at the end and lingered enough to scratch Ti-Ti's neck and allow him to raise his head to my hand, for a moment feeling a little bit of awe myself.

The Moment of Waking

MY FATHER RUMMAGED THROUGH THE TOOLBOX attached to the loader. Finally, he brought out a piece of copper wire and held it up to show me.

"Make sure to only touch the insulated part," he said, "or it will ruin your day."

His eyes had circles under them. Sometimes I heard him downstairs in the middle of the night, moving around. My father clearing his throat or the small click of the remote being set down on the coffee table were natural sounds of the evening, as much as a car passing or a dog barking somewhere in the valley. The voices from the TV were too low to make out, but enough to show that my father was awake.

He reached into the side of the engine with the wire, placing it where he had just shown me. The loader tractor was over twenty years old, and this was how it now had to be started. A spark flew and then the engine came to life.

He turned off the tractor and handed me the wire.

I held it in the middle and slowly brought it towards the starter. I let it hover between the two contact points before touching them.

"Hey!" my father yelled.

I jumped and dropped the wire.

He laughed and then rustled my hair, picking it up for me. He started the tractor himself and then tossed the wire back into the toolbox.

Every day my father limped from milking to feeding and then did whatever fieldwork he had fuel for. He walked more slowly, leaning from one side to the next, and if no one else was around sat down for a moment. He still told himself to rock 'n' roll as he worked, but sometimes it sounded like a plea. With my mother away teaching, he was often on the farm alone. The house being next to the barn, there was nowhere for him to leave his troubles behind or draw a line around them. He never got the chance to congratulate himself for surviving what he did.

In those days I had strange dreams. I would be in the milking parlor or the freestalls, or in the tiestall barn from my childhood. Usually I was with my father, but sometimes it was my grandfather instead. We were doing some act of farming: milking, feeding, delivering a calf. Nothing particularly abhorrent occurred in those dreams, but the dimensions were never quite right. The parlor was shaped in a square instead of a rectangle, or at the wrong end of the barn. The lights were dull and left us in shadow, or our shadows were long and thin and didn't always follow what we were doing. There were more cobwebs than there should be. When we spoke, we said enigmatic things to each other. There was a sense of something mean and foreboding, and it didn't seem like there was much we could do about it. We were farming, but it was an uneasy type of farming.

At the moment of waking, those dreams seemed more real and immediate than how I knew the farm to be. It took the work of a rational mind to put them back into the context of something imagined. Still, even after these images had passed, the apprehensive feeling lingered into the day. The truth beneath them remained after the particulars had been proven wrong.

The farm, as it was, already held plenty of uncomfortable details. The blades needed to be changed on the chopper, but this was expensive and had to wait. Therefore, the cows had to be given coarser silage that was lower quality. My father couldn't afford to feed grain with it. More cattle were sold. The milk check got smaller still. Every machine became rougher, more worn, and more ramshackle. The loader tractor, though, might have been the worst of them.

The steering went on it, so it feinted left and right as my father spun the wheel to compensate. The knuckle wore out on the front end, so he had to be gentle with it. My father worried about the day it would have to be replaced. The right door had been smashed off long ago when Uncle Carlton was packing the trench, and now it had a piece of hazy fiberglass bolted in its place. Because the air conditioner broke, my father removed the other door. The tractor lost the road gears and then the next fastest range. Eventually, as if it were imitating my father, it only crawled forward in slow heaves. Then, after all that, the radio quit.

Because I was there sometimes to milk those cows and run that tractor, I knew some of what my father was thinking. The things he saw around him made him feel dirty and poor. Because of the weight he carried, it felt like a punishment that he nearly wanted to deserve. Part of him thought that maybe he was, in fact, a bad farmer. He thought that maybe he didn't have the right to complain about the dairy industry because he didn't merit a place in it. Maybe he was never meant to farm. Regardless of how my father felt, however, his problems were not over yet.

We only had one neighbor. His name was Jeff and he worked at the local milk plant. Jeff was patient with what was, at times, a daily routine of one of my mother's horses getting out and marking up his lawn. If Jeff was out in his driveway, working on his truck or moving tools in his garage, my father stopped in. If it was late enough in the day he might have a beer with him. The conversation was the usual banter between neighbors—the weather, the government, local gossip. This time, however, Jeff assured my father that he had the money ready to transfer to my grandfather but was just waiting for the paperwork.

My father nodded and bit his lip, trying to give himself more time to get the joke he thought he missed. Finally, he said, "Paperwork for what?"

Jeff chuckled. "Right?" He put his hands in his pockets and rocked on his heels. He had a gym station in an old shipping container behind his house. His shoulders were broad, stretching his shirt.

My father watched Jeff.

Suddenly Jeff jerked his head back. He stared at my father with wide, searching eyes, as if to be sure. Then he raised a finger to point across the small gulley running by his lawn. "Your dad sold me that field."

My father probably blushed and then apologized, pointing out that, as Jeff probably saw himself, my grandfather was starting to get more confused lately. In any case, my grandfather couldn't have sold him the field, because the deed was in my father's name. He apologized to Jeff. There's no manual to handle aging parents, he said, but he was sorry for the hassle his father caused.

At home, although it was ridiculous, my father called the county tax office for confirmation. Then my father jumped into his pickup, slammed the door, and sped to my grandparents' house.

My grandfather had to have been quick to arrange the paralegal to drive to the hospital and get my father's signature before he might have died. There wasn't a lot of time between my father being put on a gurney and visiting hours being closed outside of immediate family. He was taken to the operating table the next morning. My grandfather didn't go to the church or the graveyard after his oldest sister's death. He didn't care what everyone else thought of him, because that was how much he hated hospitals, funerals, and anything associated with death. He didn't want to see my father before his surgery, even though the surgeon didn't expect him to live through it. My father remembered signing the paper from the paralegal, although he had trouble holding the pen. He did not stay conscious for very long, and even if he did, he could not have read anything.

What he had signed over, in the end, was the deed to his farm.

The Dennis men rarely show emotions. We use a sense of humor to deflect anything personal. Inside, however, my grandfather was filled with anger that I did not take over his farm. He saw my decision as an act of betrayal, of choosing myself over the family. My father was probably more aware of my grandfather's animosity, but I was naive to its extent. If my father died the farm would go to my mother, and by extension, to me and my sister. My grandfather wasn't going to let that happen. To him, it was now every man for himself.

My father stood in Jeff's driveway more than a year after his accident. The fact that my grandfather held onto that secret and that the weight of it did not force a confession uncloaked who he had become. That field was one of the best plots of alfalfa we had. Just as he'd done with his own farm, my grandfather had sold it for less than its value. Fortunately, Jeff allowed us to work it for free. Since it was next to his house, he bought it to make sure that the large farm would never own it and spread heavy manure there.

My grandfather couldn't afford to build a log cabin next to the pond as he had promised my grandmother. Instead, they purchased a pre-fabricated double-wide. They could have set the house to look into the valley where he had farmed, but not a single window faced that direction. Apparently, his debt followed him up the hill anyway. Selling those twenty-two acres meant that my grandfather realized that he did not have enough money.

My father kicked off his boots and yanked open the back door of my grandparents' prefab. He walked past my grandmother at the counter and ignored her greeting. There was no wall between the kitchen and the living room in the small house, so it only took him a few strides to cross onto the carpet. He stood over my grandfather.

"Something you want to tell me?" my father said, half shouting.

The Young and the Restless played on the screen in front of my grandfather. He sat in his La-Z-Boy, his elbows planted on the armrests. He didn't look at the TV, but he didn't look at my father, either. His eyes were distant, as if deep in thought.

My father stepped closer. "I can't believe you did that. You stole my farm. I can't believe it."

My grandmother stood by the counter, frozen. Her mouth hung partly open, as it tended to do as she aged. She still held an egg in her hand, her knuckles cradled around the white shell.

My grandfather folded his hands on his lap. He finally looked up to my father.

My father stood in his stained socks, one white and one gray. His jeans had a hole in them, the frayed threads white where Chlorox used to disinfect udders had splashed. "Land taxes are due. You better pay them, since you own the land now." My father threw up his arms, a gesture very unlike him.

My father could have called a lawyer and had the signature on the transfer invalidated, and maybe even had my grandfather charged with fraud. However, it took every dollar coming in from the farm and my mother's income to make it through a day, and that still wasn't enough. He didn't have the money to retain a lawyer. He knew that my grandfather wouldn't pay the taxes and that the land would be gone.

"I can't believe you'd do that," my father said. "After everything."

My grandfather might have thought that he meant after my father's accident and the problems with the bank. Instead, it was more likely the years they spent farming. They shared together more than most fathers and sons did, and because of it, had a relationship many would envy. My father took one final look at my grandfather, calculating the loss that he had stumbled upon.

The door banged shut behind him.

My father later said that his mistake was believing that my grandfather's lawyer was also his lawyer and that he represented both of their interests. Instead, that lawyer helped my grandfather look out for himself. Apparently, there were meetings my father didn't know about. Ultimately, however, my father's mistake was more tragic: he cared more for my grandfather than my grandfather did for him. If my father had followed the bank's advice and had my grandfather declared unfit, my grandfather would never have had the chance to steal the land.

My father was confident that my grandfather intended to sell our farm regardless of the result of the surgery. My father would have come out of the hospital to find someone else in our fields. He always believed that it was the act of so many people coming together to keep the farm going that kept my grandfather from daring to go through with it.

In the end, my grandparents' debts and liens became my parents' problems. They had to find ways to pay for things that weren't theirs, and with money they didn't have. They couldn't put my grandfather in a nursing home because the government would repossess all the land in his name to fund it. Much like with the bank, they were in danger of losing everything.

My father was the only one who could say how my grandfather's actions near the end of his life recast the years before it. The question will always remain of how much of my grandfather after his head injury in 2001 was actually him. It draws out even small moments of selfishness from the past when my grandfather put himself first. We used to laugh at the fact that my parents had to end their honeymoon early because my grandfather called to say he needed help chopping corn, or that he told my father that he couldn't play baseball growing up because farmers' sons had to be in the field in the spring, my father eventually finding the baseball trophy in the school with my grandfather's name on it. Maybe we are all inclined to self-interest and it only takes an unfortunate moment to unearth it. Maybe my grandfather's behavior was entirely clinical and not his fault at all. Despite what anyone may have thought of my grandfather at that time, Andrew Dennis was still living and breathing and driving his old Dodge around the block. He carried the name that was on the deed to the farm. Therefore, my father's byline changed once more: he had his income taken away for eight months, then had to learn to walk again, and then was betrayed by his father.

Some nights I woke to the howling of coyotes. Our house was in the bottom of a valley and sound carried through gullies from miles away. Their calls in the darkness sometimes merged with feverish yipping that meant they were closing in on their prey. Whatever they were chasing would soon be surrounded and overwhelmed. It was impossible to tell which fields or woods it was happening in. The ominous sounds drifted through the open bedroom window to reach me in my sleep.

My father would probably be awake downstairs. He always spent part of the night in the armchair. He'd flip through the channels until he found an old movie, and if he didn't, took a DVD out of the drawer. If I went downstairs to piss, he'd ask me if the TV was too loud, and I'd tell him that it wasn't. Sometimes I sat on the couch and watched the movie with him for a while before going back to bed.

Later, my mother told me that in the first few years of their marriage, my father would have breakfast with my grandfather. He would go to my grandparents' at 2:30 in the morning and eat sausage and pancakes. Afterwards, he came back to our house to start the milking. I believe my father thought about that sometimes while the TV flickered pale light over him.

My father had nightmares for two years after the accident. He would often wake up just as the arms of the skid steer came down on him. Other times he felt the pain of his vertebrae snapping all over again. He never said if he used to scream when that happened, nor did my mother. Even after the night terrors subsided, he still often woke up with the anxious feeling that he had to go out and milk and that he had forgotten that somehow.

Eventually my father went back to bed, too, or maybe fell asleep in the chair while the movie played. The pain in his body made it difficult to sleep for long. After a few hours, his back became sore, no matter how he lay. Sometimes there wasn't anything else he could do except sit in the dark and wait for the morning milking.

Delayed Portents

AFTER I GOT MY MASTER'S, my father started giving me time to write when I was home. If he had to do something that he could do alone, he told me to stay in the house and that he could handle it. Sometimes, when he got to the part where he needed an extra pair of hands to lift something or hold it in place, he would open the back door and call out my name, and then encourage me to go inside once the task was finished. It was his way of showing that he took my ambitions for myself seriously. Considering how he grew up, where he was given little space to do anything but farm, it was progressive. He didn't want the farm to feel like a prison where I couldn't do what I needed to. After returning to Iowa, I was always coming and leaving, and part of him might have been afraid that there would be a day when I stopped coming back.

It was late November, and after an unusually warm month, the temperature changed. My room was small and John Deere green, because at the age of twelve or thirteen that was the color I wanted. It had no heat and got cold in the winter. When I was at my desk, I turned on a portable radiator for a few minutes at a time. The windows were frosted and had dead flies beneath them.

I fidgeted every time the tractor started in the driveway. It was an uncomfortable feeling to be on the farm and know that work was being done, and not be a part of it. It seemed contrary to what it meant to be a good person. Sometimes I got up and went to the window to watch my father pass by with a bale for the dry cows or to spread a load of manure. Then I sat back down and stared at the notebook in front of me.

With my mother at work and my sister married and moved away, my father was usually alone during the day. Having someone in the parlor during the morning and night milking, as well as to eat lunch with, probably meant more to him than any other way I could have been useful. To cover the things I needed, I often took on poorly paid freelance work, from writing dog food descriptions to giving reviews for hotels I had never been in. These opportunities were the result of a nascent internet and allowed me to use the phrase "I'm working" while at my desk. Still, if a visitor stopped by the house, I felt eccentric and lazy coming down the stairs, revealing that I was not in the barn.

Outside the window, snow flurries were pulled sideways across the glass. In addition to the heater, I also had a blanket on my lap. There was usually another sweatshirt next to the chair, for when the cold settled into me. My desk had belonged to my great-great-grandfather Oscar, dating it to sometime in the 1800s. It was at my grandparents' house, and when they gave it to me, told me not to tell my aunts and uncles, because they wanted the desk, too.

I don't know anything about Oscar or what people might have thought about him. I assume he did some farming, because most people did back then. I wondered what type of Dennis he was. Was he loyal and patient or did he have a self-serving streak? Was he more bookish than the rest of the family? I wondered what traits I eventually got from him. Maybe all our troubles, in a way that we didn't know, could ultimately be traced to him.

Downstairs, the back door opened. If my father was coming in for lunch, the next sound would be his boots pried off on the doorframe and then picked up and put inside. This time, however, I knew he was leaning on the handle because he shouted into the house: "Ryan, come here."

When I came down the steps he said, "See this." I grabbed my coat off a hook and slipped on my boots, following him out to the porch.

We looked past our woodpile to the sky overhead. Hundreds of Canada geese circled against the slate background. They turned above us, slowly, in a slurry of gray and black feathers. The wind threw their blatting sounds around them.

"Poor bastards," my father said. "They're not going to make it."

The sky was loud and full of panic. The geese flew in one direction, splitting off and later merging again, and then flew another way, as if the horizon trapped them. We agreed that the warm weather had confused them, and they hadn't gone south when they were supposed to. Now they weren't going to live.

It seemed the geese didn't know anything else to do but keep flying. Their insistent calls fell heavily over us. We put our hand in our pockets to warm them and gazed past our own breath. It was hard to watch, and at the same time difficult to go back into the house.

"That's heartbreaking," my father said, and then surprised me by saying, "Remember this. Remember this so you can write about it someday."

A few hours later, I came back to the porch in my socks and the geese were still above the tree line. Their wings beat against the slow flurries around them, their necks straining forward. They stretched below the clouds, their bodies heaving, keeping a pulsing shape. They continued to turn above the dry cow pasture and the gulley in front of us as the sky darkened, until the night took them.

Notes on the American Dairy Industry

THE FOUNDING OF A NATION REQUIRES A MYTHOLOGY to sustain it, especially in its early years. America did not have the cultural centers of London and Paris, but it did have plenty of farmers. Thomas Jefferson's claim that "those who labor in the earth are the chosen people of God" persisted for centuries.

Jefferson's agrarianism is more complicated than it seems. He may have believed the cultivators of the earth to be more virtuous and independent than other people, but he wasn't including women and people of color. Still, the notion had its uses at times, both political and personal. After a tough day pulling a calf or getting a wagon unstuck, at least we knew we were the backbone of the country.

However, agricultural policy began encouraging cheaper food instead of sustainable farming. Politicians, farm journals, and news sources lauded the reach of American agriculture across the world, ignoring that the farmers themselves struggled. Whether John Deere, Monsanto, Pioneer, or Cargill, the bigger the American companies were, the more they were to be celebrated. As the twenty-first century continued, it became clear that no one had chosen us at all. Instead, America deferred to another entity to be its champion, and that was the corporation.

Consolidation among agribusiness limited options and drove up costs for farmers in all sectors. One example consequential to dairy farming was the price of seed. According to a report by American Progress, in 2015 the four largest biotech companies controlled 85 percent of the corn seed market. Not only did farmers have fewer purchasing choices in the twenty-first century, but the cost of corn seed rose 259 percent from 1995 to 2011. Additionally, Monsanto—now owned by Bayer—made farmers sign a "technology agreement" that prevented them from saving some of their harvest to plant the following year. Having few alternatives in the marketplace and being reliant on the yields of genetically modified corn to stay competitive, farmers were forced to buy expensive seed every season.

From dairy manufacturers to retailers, consolidation in the farming industry has further squeezed the producer. However, the most detrimental—and baffling—example especially illustrates the standing of the American dairy farmer. In 1922, Congress passed the Capper–Volstead Act, allowing antitrust exemptions for farm cooperatives. The legislation was meant to support small independent farmers in a market where they had little power. A century later, the law still remains in place. However, instead of protecting farmers, it has created one of their biggest problems.

In 1998, Dairy Farmers of America (DFA) was formed by the merger of four dairy cooperatives: the southern region of Associated Milk Producers, Inc. (AMPI); Mid-America Dairymen, Inc.; Milk Marketing, Inc. (MMI); and Western Dairymen Cooperative, Inc. Since then, they have absorbed numerous other cooperatives. The amalgamation was billed as a move to give dairy farmers more voice in national policy-making and greater agency in the market. DFA now controls substantially more milk than any other cooperative and with margins that grow every year.

Farmers who made up DFA membership became puzzled when their cooperative began acquiring processing plants. The purpose of the co-op was to negotiate with the processors to make sure that the farmer received a fair price for milk, and now DFA had an interest in keeping the milk price low in order to profit in the manufacturing sector. DFA continued its vertical integration, developing ventures in everything from testing to hauling, forcing its members to use their services and weakening competition. The culmination of DFA's monopsony included Dean Foods, for which they orchestrated mergers to give the giant food processor a leading share of milk sales in many regional markets—and then made deals with Dean to make DFA its sole supplier. In 2020, DFA purchased Dean Foods, giving it complete dominance over the milk industry.

Dairy Farmers of America experienced lavish profits while the milk price fell to historic lows. Due to exemptions under the Capper–Volstead Act, DFA is not required to share its earnings with stakeholders, nor does it have to report them. It had been uncovered that only a quarter of profits get paid to farmers annually, as well as that the dairy co-op makes 60 percent of its income from nonmember business dealings. DFA is also exempted from disclosing the salary of the board, but the *New York Times* reported that Gary Hanman, founder of DFA, made $31 million over seven years and had access to a private jet. In 2017, DFA moved into new $30 million headquarters, at which the art and decor cost $1.5 million alone. During all of this, dairy executives who partnered with DFA on certain investments saw incredible returns, sometimes 20 to 150 times what they bankrolled. This occurred while dairy farmers were going out of business in record numbers.

In the end, there was no appetite for protecting the family dairy farm against the interests of corporations. Instead, dairy farmers were punished for not getting bigger themselves. In 2014, the United States discontinued the Milk Income Loss Contract, which provided payment support when the milk price got too low. The MILC had favored family farms because only a limited number of pounds was covered annually. It was replaced with the Margin Protection Program, in which all farmers received "catastrophic coverage" and had the opportunity to buy additional insurance. It was a cost harder to bear by family farms, and many couldn't afford the extra coverage.

From 2003 to 2020, 40,000 dairy farms went out of business in the United States. That loss was not inevitable. There was no law of nature that suggested that it was better to milk more cows. Neither God nor

Mother Earth asked for it. Instead, certain men decided it themselves. It's not on account of technology, because having bigger tractors didn't mean that we had to use them to tear up the land. It's not that we have to feed more people, because there are mountains of butter and dry powder in storage sheds and farmers are often asked to dump their milk because the co-ops don't need it. It isn't what we learned from our fathers, because our fathers never milked 500, then 1,000, then 5,000 cows. It is not the simple nature of economics because economics is not nature, but a game mankind made up with his own rules. If there is anything natural about farm economics, we would have recognized the cost of agribusiness and large farming on the environment, rural communities, and our understanding of ourselves. Through the years, many people have shrugged their shoulders and said that they hate to see small farmers go out of business, but that's just how the world works. However, that is not true. Instead, the world was working just fine before farming got big.

IV.
The Problem with Endings

Seasons of the Absurd

WHEN RUST FIRST APPEARED ON THE TAILGATE, he put a Superman decal over it. It gave us something to pick on him about. After the bumper rotted away, he dragged out a beam of reinforced steel he had lying around the shop and welded it in its place. The holes in the bed or the wheel casing didn't bother him much, because even though it was my father's only way of getting around when my mother took the car to work, it was still a farm truck. All its roughness fit what was expected of it. Then, however, the brakes went. My father couldn't afford to fix them, but he still needed a truck.

Our farm is in a dip between hills. Whatever direction a vehicle is coming from, it is coasting down a steep slope. My father held his work shoe over the brake at the top of the hill and still, by the time he reached the bottom, he'd have to violently swing the Chevy into the turn and hope that no cars were coming. Sometimes they were. My father would either have to freewheel past our driveway and go to the top of the next hill to try again, or cut in front of oncoming traffic. He drove slowly when going through town and anticipated the traffic lights a hundred yards ahead, and then waved the times he got it wrong and passed through the red light. He didn't tell many people about the truck, because it would seem crazy to anyone else. And although it was crazy, it was the reality my family lived in.

Everyone who knew that my father drove the Chevy without brakes knew what was going to happen, Superman decal or not. My father probably knew it too, even if he didn't feel like there was much he could do to stop it.

My parents were heading to town to do their weekend grocery

shopping. My mother's car, without four-wheel drive, must have been dubious on that winter day. The wind on our hill drags snow across the fields and onto the pavement, whether or not it is snowing. The snowplow is less diligent when the school bus doesn't pass by, and in the countryside, it can be hit-or-miss anyway.

My father put the truck in its lowest gear and started up the road. It fishtailed slightly but he didn't take the foot off the gas, knowing it is almost impossible to restart on a snowy hill. The motor became louder as it worked harder. Both of my parents were silent. A breeze whirled a mist of snow outside the window. The tops of the pine trees swayed around them. My father rubbed the dashboard and winked at my mother.

The old Chevy slowed as it climbed, and then the back end started swinging. Knowing my father, he turned the radio off as he tried to compensate with the steering wheel. My father probably talked to the truck, while my mother probably yelled at my father. The top of the hill is deceptively far away—one might think they've made it when they crested the steepest part, but there is still another hundred yards of incline. The engine groaned as the wheels began turning freely, kicking snow behind them. Eventually the truck slowed to a stop.

My parents looked at each other.

And then the Chevy went backwards.

The sound of the snow crunching beneath the worn tires raised in pitch as the truck picked up speed. The whine of the transmission grew louder too. My father looked over his shoulder and steered, watching the next hill in the distance for oncoming traffic. As the Chevy gained momentum it became harder to keep on the road, let alone on his side of it. I don't know if they made promises to God or each other in that moment, but either would have been quick because they were moving backwards fast. There was a small gravel pull-off above one of our fields where the county sometimes left equipment. My father had a hurried decision to make: try to hit that short driveway or take his chances in our lawn at the bottom of the hill.

He whipped the truck around and timed it well enough to make the county's parking spot. My parents exhaled and congratulated each other. My father laughed out loud. He probably said something under-stated like, "Well, that was interesting," while my mother would have used the Lord's name in vain. While all this was going on, however, the truck kept rolling. My father instinctively hit the brake, which did nothing more than provide a sense of irony as the wheels still turned. They kept going, in fact, leaving tracks in the snow, until the Chevy rolled into a ravine.

My parents walked to the house without saying anything. When they arrived, my father took the tractor and chains and pulled the Chevy out of the gulley. Then he called a mechanic to pick up the truck. He decided to find the money for brakes somewhere.

The seasons came and went as they always had, but now they were delicate. The work they required only got done by giving up something else. Fence posts were pulled from one field, straightened, and put into another. The side of the barn had sheets of corrugated steel that had slid off the roof and were half-buried in the mud. The tractors we drove smoked or overheated or couldn't stop with weight behind them. From a distance, it probably seemed absurd. We always knew that no one was going to save us. We were starting to realize, however, that we couldn't save ourselves.

Sometimes, in the milking parlor, we found corn at the bottom of our coffee cups. It meant that manure had splattered into them. It used to be that getting kernels in our teeth would make us gag and laugh and tease each other. In that period, however, we just turned the mug over and continued working. During the milking, my father sometimes chewed an unlit cigar. He kept it in the metal box that held the sleeve filters for the milk pump. He was never tempted to light it, but instead slowly ground it into grizzle and spit it into the grates.

My father's body hurt. The doctors told him it would only get worse. I don't know if they gave him an estimate or not, but my father knew he wouldn't live as long as other people. He only had was what was in front of him. From it, he took stories. That winter, he accidentally shot a deer in the leg while hunting. He described the deer trying to hobble away and my father limping after it as the slowest chase ever. He confessed to unhooking a wagon and turning around to find it gone, because it had rolled into another field. He told everyone at the pond about the Chevy and they all laughed. My father realized that we didn't live in seasons or days anymore but instead moments.

He helped me see it for myself, too. Late in summer, the transition from baling hay to chopping corn was made awkward by bad weather and being behind in fieldwork. The stalks of reed canary were dry and bent towards the ground. The first cutting that remained had grown coarse, the yellowing grass bright against the murky horizon. The air stood heavy, suspending small insects that dully turned in circles. My father drove through the field with the pickup, trying to get me excited about mowing old hay before the imminent thunderstorm.

"Relax and enjoy it," he said. "It's better than milking."

I looked up at the sky.

Our self-propelled New Holland was modern when it was purchased twenty-some years ago. My father kept it in good shape, partly because it was his favorite machine. The seat sat high above the hay and the cab had air-conditioning and the last cassette player on the farm. Singers from the nineties were often piled under Emily while she watched the wheels turn. While I was in high school, the local gas station started selling old country cassettes for two dollars apiece, and one by one I bought most of them. Every time I cut hay, I brought a few more with me and afterward took a couple back to the house.

We were in The Field Past the Pond. The dirt road that ran parallel to it was seasonally maintained, extending beyond the hedgerow and out of sight towards a woods and a hinterland where those who live there do not want to be noticed. I had heard my grandfather say that in one of the nearby hedgerows was a stone benchmark with an elevation figure and a claim to be the highest point in the county. I never found that stone, but looking around I could see nothing taller than the tops of the trees across the road. Below the field stretched the valley. I was, as far as I could tell, the last thing between the earth and the sky.

When I was growing up, my father was patient in showing me how to do fieldwork. He would go around the field once, the tractor pulling whatever machine I hadn't used before, and then stop to change seats with me. He would make a few comments, correcting me or offering advice, and then eventually rest the side of his head against the window. Sometimes he closed his eyes, and I think he pretended to be asleep so I wouldn't get as nervous. Soon, though, he would walk back to the barn and leave me to finish the field.

My right palm rested on the haybine's throttle, my fingers slipping into the wear marks left by my father's hand. I kept my thumb below the toggle switch needed to raise the blades. Dark patches of weeds sometimes signaled a woodchuck hole. The heads of timothy swayed in front of the rotating blades as I neared them in the haybine. Red-winged blackbirds flew above in small circles over the grass in various corners of the field. Leafhoppers crawled along the window, sometimes flinging themselves into the breeze.

The wind swept through the hay, twisting the grass at its roots. It carried with it the smell of the weather about to change as it loosened the empty seed hulls from the head of the haybine and tossed them around the outside of the cab. The end of a cassette stuck out of the tape deck, shaking. Emily lay on the floor in the corner, looking past her own image to the ground beneath. Her tail collected dust from the wrenches and grease cans under the seat. I stared into the grass as well, beyond the stalks and tops of hay to look for the shapes of stones that might lie below.

A dark silhouette crossed in front of me. Watching the ground, I saw it only out of the corner of my eye. The second barn swallow swung and dipped through the air with sharp precision. It skimmed the top of the windrow before circling behind me. Suddenly, others cut through the breeze with their pointed wings, plunging, lifting, but where they could have emerged from in the open plain I did not know. The machine crept forward as the air grew thick with the shadows of birds intersecting in jagged flight. I pulled the brake and descended the steps.

Barn swallows are common before a storm, but I had never seen so many. They flashed in swooping arcs over one another, creating a shifting lattice on the gray horizon. They skimmed the top of grass, bending past each other. There was no way to tell how many there were, but there seemed to be hundreds. Their tail feathers flickered like static over the landscape. They looped around me and the machine I stood next to, silent except for the sound made by their wings carving the wind. One of them was on course for my face. I ducked, but at the last minute it lifted above me, flashing the creamy feathers on its breast. I laughed for the sheer excitement of it.

Suddenly there was something beautiful about cutting hay that was going to be rained on. The futility didn't take away from it. I chose, for the first time in a long time, to see myself not between anything, but in a moment and place on its own.

The Food Bank

ONCE OR TWICE A DAY, we could hear the slow approach of my grandfather's Gator as it passed the house. He drove around the block of dirt roads by our land. If we were in the lawn, he waved to us, hunched over the steering wheel. Occasionally, he had my grandmother's Bichon Frise on his lap, the dog lifting its nose to lick the draft.

This time he pulled into our driveway.

My grandfather seldom went into our house. If he did, he would call for my father from the back room.

My grandfather stood there with his hands on his hips, staring at our linoleum. He didn't look up at my father.

"Want a cup of coffee?" my father asked.

"We need money for food."

Life had carried on, regardless of what my grandfather had done. A month later my father started talking to him again, and eventually we visited their house like we had before. Sometimes it seems like that doesn't make sense. Other times, when I think about it, I realize that it couldn't have gone differently. Part of it was the nature of the farm, and the other part the nature of the people around it. Since the nineties, farming had been made up of having to face one hardship after another, and farmers like my father had to learn how to reset themselves each time. Being civil again was an act of survival, because there was too much else going on. Figuring out how to pay for teat dip and hot water was hard enough. There wasn't enough left of my father for him to explore his anger.

As far as I know, my grandmother was unaware of the decisions my grandfather made after his accident, and she only vaguely deduced them after they happened. This ignorance might have become willful at some point, affording her the ability to separate herself from his financial worries and the scorn he drew. If she was kept out of his dealings her whole life, she wasn't going to step in and defend him now.

My grandmother was also prematurely aging, forgetting words and calling people by the wrong name. She quit reading and later her driving became dangerous. Ultimately, however, my grandmother had more acumen than my grandfather. That might have swung the power balance in her favor for the first time. She had depended on my grandfather to provide security and certain material comforts that she could look forward to in retirement age. Instead, there wasn't much waiting for them in their final years.

My grandparents could have brought their furniture and beds from their old house to the prefab on the hill. Instead, my grandmother left them there and bought everything new again, spending ten thousand dollars. It wasn't the type of thing she would have done earlier. Worse still, after the furniture was delivered, she decided that she didn't like it and gave it away, ordering new couches and beds again.

In addition to whatever Social Security my grandparents were entitled to from the government, my parents paid my grandfather $500 every month for the thirty-seven cows my father had gotten from him. Without mortgages or loans in their names, my grandparents didn't have many expenses. What my parents didn't find out until a few years later was that my grandfather had also taken my father's retirement from the co-op. Dairy Farmers of America, who sold our milk, set aside a part of every check towards a retirement payment for the farmer. My father's and grandfather's farms were under the same account. My father had been milking his own cows for over thirty years when my grandfather sold out. My grandfather took the retirement savings for both himself and my father and didn't tell anyone.

My parents never entirely knew where the money went that they had given to my grandparents. They saw glimpses of squandering, such as my grandfather going to town to buy hundreds of dollars' worth of stones for my grandmother's flower bed, or paying someone to have the new kitchen painted again. For a while, my grandfather claimed that the contractor who sold him the prefab house was cheating him and making him finance the building a second time, but that seemed unlikely. All my parents knew was that thousands of dollars had somehow passed through my grandparents' hands.

My father stood in the doorway of our house and shrugged. "We have no money."

Even with all the sacrifices my father had made for my grandfather in the years that led to this moment, if my father had twenty dollars in his wallet, he would have given it to him. Instead, a father and son stood facing each other with nothing between them but unkind history.

Someone else might have been filled with righteous anger. Few people would have resisted saying, "I told you so," or "Look at you now." I wasn't there, and when I learned about it, I knew I would have been one of those people. However, my father didn't do that. Considering how many of his decisions came from love for my grandfather, this moment probably hurt him. Having to be a parent to my grandfather reinforced the fatality of what he and my father once had.

"Take what you need out of the cellar freezer," my father said, closing the door.

The Milkman

Wʜᴇɴ I ᴡᴀs ᴛᴡᴇʟᴠᴇ, I liked getting up at 5:30 to milk. The quietness of the morning matched something inside of me. I started drinking coffee then, because it seemed right. My father would pull on his jeans and tell me to take my time, but I followed him out anyway. Walking through the dark before the sun rose made it feel like we were one step ahead of the world.

Instead, in my mid to late twenties, and in the farming that occurred then, the mornings often felt less like a new opening than the continuation of yesterday's dilemmas. On days like those, it was hard to convince ourselves that we were working towards anything other than staving off bigger fears for a little longer. Because my father didn't answer their phone calls, more bill collectors pulled into our barn's driveway. My father didn't bother to avoid them anymore, but met them in the milk house, and without expression, asked how they were doing. Sometimes he turned over a five-gallon bucket and sat on it. He nodded and stared into the distance as the bill collector explained that my father was behind and that they needed a payment. He looked like a child being admonished.

At one point Ti-Ti started getting beat up by another tom. Ti-Ti would wait until the other cats had left the milk dish and limp up to it to lick the metal. He didn't have the aggression of other males, and while others would have left for somewhere else, he remained in the corner of the barn, tucked into himself.

One morning the .22 was leaning outside the parlor door. It looked feral and out of place there. Although I assumed it wasn't loaded, I glanced at it every time I passed by, as if it would suddenly tip over and fire. A few days later, I was feeding calves when my father came up to me, holding a dead tom cat by its tail.

"He's not going to bother Ti-Ti anymore."

There were plenty of signs showing how my father was feeling, if you knew how to read them.

After my grandfather's farm had been sold, my father started going to the barn later. It didn't happen at once but seemed to be a change that stretched over several years. The first few times that we left the house half an hour or hour later it probably felt like a novelty, a stolen pleasure. Then, however, it became more usual. Eventually, we saw the sun rise in front of the kitchen window, which was unnatural to the shape of our day. It didn't fit with how I knew my father to be. I offered to get the milking started by myself, but he told me to sit down and relax.

My father was resolute in smiling. I wished that going to the barn later didn't mean anything. My grandfather fell out of sync with the rhythms of farming, and he deteriorated with his farm. We watched it happen together. Now my father was misaligned with the repetitions that had defined his life.

Until that point, we had a good relationship with whatever milkman was on our route. It was important because they read the milk weights, determining how much a farmer was paid. Sometimes, when Grandma Dennis gave me a bag of cookies to take home, my father made sure I left a few for the milkman. My grandfather always told about the milkman he once had who admitted he had been shorting him a hundred pounds every day and giving it to my grandfather's brother. Milkmen were a source of gossip and banter, but had, ultimately, twenty dollars' worth of power each pickup in the numbers they wrote down.

For many years we had a good milkman named Hayes. He passed away suddenly from cancer, however, at the age of sixty. I wrote a memorial piece for him in *Progressive Dairyman*, which they framed and hung up at the hauling company.

The man who replaced him was named Tuckerson.

Having to follow Hayes was not enviable, and Tuckerson might have gotten heckled about it in the truck garage. He might have gotten picked on for much of his life, for all we knew, or had trouble talking with people. More importantly, I believed him when he said that if he couldn't finish his route before nine am he would have to wait in line at the milk plant for two or three hours longer. Unfortunately for him, though, he started picking up our milk during a bad period for my father.

It started off as dirty looks by Tuckerson as he leaned on the truck's tank. Sometimes he cleared his throat while he waited for my father to switch the pipes in the milk house after the milking. They didn't talk about the weather or about what other farmers were doing. Tuckerson didn't get any cookies. In the past, my father would leave a little milk in the reading tube when he checked the milk weights, making it obvious to the milkman that he had seen them too. Now my father stood over Tuckerson and watched him record the figure.

Tuckerson had been a milkman for a while, presumably. He knew how to get under a farmer's skin. He started showing up at the milking and standing at the top of the parlor.

My father and Tuckerson might have made strained conversation sometimes, but mostly they were silent. To ignore someone was difficult for my father, which belied just how much of an escalation it was for Tuckerson to be in the parlor. It was an aggressive act and the message was clear: if my father didn't want him there, he should get the milking done sooner.

The presence of Tuckerson in our parlor continued for a while. He walked in towards the last cows to hurry the milking. Eventually I thought my father would say, "To hell with it," and go to the barn earlier. There was plenty to do, and the extra time in the morning could be used for anything, even a longer breakfast. However, that's not what happened.

One morning, it was once again getting close to eight o'clock before we went to the barn. Then it went past eight. My father still stared at the television screen, watching a police drama. It was the weekend, so my mother milked with us. If she had mentioned in private that we should begin the workday, the suggestion was not heeded. I slipped on the dirty pair of jeans I was going to milk in and then sat back down. A few cattle called out from under the tin roof, confused by still being in their stalls. The kitchen was flooded in daylight that fell on the farming journals and unopened bills that covered the table. Finally, the show ended. My father rose to fill his coffee cup again and then trudged out to the barn.

It was the latest we had ever started the morning milking. So late, in fact, that Tuckerson's rig was already parked next to the milk house.

Tuckerson glared at us as we passed the hood of the milk truck. I didn't know if my father acknowledged Tuckerson sitting behind the steering wheel, because I didn't dare look up from the ground. Even though I wasn't directly implicated, I still felt the weight of the standoff. I would not be surprised, though, if my mother waved to Tuckerson ironically, or at least smiled.

I've heard farmers say, parsing their situation, that they get it from all sides. They name things like markets, banks, the weather, bill collectors, and lawyers. At this point, all or most of these things were already hard on my father. That milking was probably similar to the thousands of other milkings on thousands of other mornings. The only thing different was that there was a tension building in him. The fact that he was not one to show his internal weather did not mean that it was not there. In the end, it was not that he felt like he was wronged by the milkman Tuckerson, but only that Tuckerson provided him a face for all that was wrong with farming.

Tuckerson was hot by the time we finished milking, having had the chance to sit in the cab of his truck and think about it.

My father pushed open the milk house door with the toe of his boot and walked out with two buckets of milk for the calf hutches. My mother allowed it to swing onto her hip as she followed behind him with a set of bottles and nipples. The milk truck sat in the driveway, Tuckerson's thick arm hanging out the open window. The image of my parents flickered back at them in the curve of the steel tank, oblong and distorted. Tuckerson pointed at my father as he passed.

"Would it honestly kill you to get done by eight-thirty?" Tuckerson had a round, fleshy face. He kept a toothpick in the back of his teeth, flicking his tongue off it now and then.

My father didn't break stride with the buckets. He didn't look up at the truck heaving on its tires or at Tuckerson in the driver's seat.

Tuckerson gripped the wheel. Dark blotches appeared on his cheeks and neck. "You need to step things up. Everyone else gets done on time," he said, slapping his palm against the outside of the door.

"Fuck you," my father said.

My father had always been easygoing. It made people like him. He was not one to get offended, and in that era of farming keeping an even keel was necessary to survive. He had been accused, often by my mother and sometimes by his children in our lesser moments, of being a push-over. This stayed with him. Once, when someone called him laid-back, he later chafed at the remark, saying, "Laid-back? I'm not laid-back." More importantly on this morning, however, was that he was feeling particularly powerless against a father who could no longer reason. He was in a situation that working harder couldn't fix, and the answer wasn't in front of him. For now, regardless of everything else, this was my father's moment. He had told our milkman to fuck himself.

Tuckerson bit on his toothpick. His hand outside the truck made a fist. "At least you won't be on my route for too long. I can't see this place lasting much longer." He looked around and added, "Since you're such a slatherass."

Only my father knew what his response was going to be.

My mother quickly stepped in front of him. She stuck her index finger into the space of the open window and shook it at Tuckerson. "Don't you talk to my husband like that," she said, her teeth clenched.

I was around the corner of the barn, feeding calves at the time. I didn't see the confrontation, only the milk truck bounding down the driveway without our milk in it. Instead, my father described it to me, partly crestfallen.

"I can't deny that it was emasculating," he said, recounting how his showdown was usurped by my mother. Even though he was glad that my mother defended him, it was clear that he wanted this one for himself. "I guess that was just the woman I married," he finally said, half-curious and half-proud. The exchange wasn't any better for Tuckerson in the end, either. Once he reached the top of the hill, he called the hauling company and explained what happened. They told him to go back and collect our milk.

Part of me thought that if we could just keep the same relentless routine, then we would be okay. Perhaps if we worked as if nothing had changed then maybe any change wouldn't be that much of a problem. However, my responsibilities were only the tasks I was given, and only when I was home. My father, who had the farm on his shoulders, was starting to realize that everything was not going to be all right.

When Fish Eat

Whenever I came home, my father made sure I enjoyed it. He might have thought that if I liked being there, I would be more likely to move back, or at least keep visiting. More than that, though, was his tendency to take care of the people around him and make sure they were happy. One of the things I liked the most when I went home was to go fly-fishing on the river.

Hunting stories were a currency in Allegany County. A person talked about the size of the buck they got for most of the year. All the men in our family hunted. I did, too, but wasn't good at it.

In seventh grade, I picked up a copy of *A River Runs Through It* that was lying on a classroom radiator. The first paragraph was about a boy growing up with religion and fly-fishing, and how, in his family, there was little distinction between the two. The sentences were short and elegant. Something about them struck me in a way that is rare for an adolescent. I put the book down, bought a fly rod, and learned how to fly-fish before reading the rest of it.

As far as anyone knew, I was only person in our family to ever fly-fish. Grandma Dennis's father died well before I was born, and the fact that he was an avid fisherman was one of the few things I knew about him. However, it was understood that he used bait and went to lakes. Perhaps it was its middle-class connotations that kept fly-fishing out of our family, or maybe it was just that no one's father had done it before them. After growing up with a pond, however, there was something novel about moving water.

My hands were not good with tools, but a fly rod is simple and meticulous. It still required precision—in the shape of the line, in laying the fly on the water, in keeping the line tight—as well as patience after the fly tangles into the tippet. It was a quietly relentless pursuit. The rhythm in casting a line was not entirely different from the pulse of the milkers in the parlor, except that it happened on a river.

A friend of the family took me to the Genesee the first few summers, teaching me how to read the water and tie a cinch knot. Eventually, though, my father asked me to show him the spots on the river where I fished. We'd pull in next to a bridge a few hours before dusk. The fish were more active just after dawn and right before dark. My father often repeated what he had heard from his grandfather, which was that the unfortunate part of fishing was that fish eat at the same time as cows. There were plenty of ways that the farm needed to be caught up. Grandpa Dennis, the man who asked my father to come home from his honeymoon early to chop corn, never hesitated to get work out of him. My father could have asked me to stay back and help out that evening, and it wouldn't have bothered me much. Instead, my father joined me.

We usually went to Weidrick Bridge. I liked it because it had different types of water: slow and deep, currents churning into pools, and a weir that turned over oxygen and attracted larger trout. We parked along the shoulder of the road and pushed our way through the brush until we got to the stream. My father carried a tackle box and a cottage cheese container of worms that he found under old silage plastic. He set them in the grass and fished from the bank after I went up the river.

For a while, my father would cast the bobber and worm upstream, watch it drift by him, and then cast again. Sometimes Grandpa Kramer went as well and they would chat to each other, occasionally rebaiting the hooks after they were cleaned by the fingerling bass along the shore. If my father was alone, he would stare across the water as the red and white float passed through his vision. He was naturally restless, and his accident made it difficult to sit for long anyway. He would get up and stand for a while with his hands in his pockets, and maybe tell the fish to start biting. Eventually my father would reel in the line and set the pole in the weeds, and then walk along the edge slowly.

Sometimes my father watched me for a while before I noticed him. I would be staring at the fly and insulated by the sounds of the stream moving against rocks. When I looked over, he would wave me off and say to keep fishing. He sat with his elbows on his knees, absently pulling at the goldenrod around him. Sometimes he balled up the leaves and tossed them in the water. My father never tried to force me into his image. He didn't insist that I be like everyone else in the family. That was the way he was different from those who came before him. Instead, he would sit on the bank and watch me fish until it grew dark.

An Ending, Mostly Chosen

THERE WAS A REFRAIN THAT FOLLOWED my grandfather's accident. My father repeated it every time my grandfather came into conversation: I wish you knew him back then.

In the eighties, the government provided commodity loans and used the shelled corn a farmer had in storage as collateral. Each farmer was offered a certificate that they could exchange for loan repayment if they didn't want to sell their corn. The program was implemented to reduce the oversupply of corn, as well as give the producer more options in the market. Some local farmers, however, did not understand the system behind the certificates and sold them to my grandfather, with a small profit to the farmer. My grandfather was able to use these certificates to pay off his loans and make extra income for himself.

The Corps of Engineers owned a large plot of gravel fields outside of Canaseraga. In the mid-1970s the land went up for rent.

The fields the Dennises farmed were hill ground. There's a joke about hill farmers always being poor, but there's also truth to it. Hill ground stays wet longer, is harder to work, and is usually less productive. My grandfather recognized the value of the Corps of Engineers' fields and convinced his brother Carlton to lease them with him. The typical rent for land back then was $15–$20 per acre. My grandfather bid $35.

Carlton quit farming soon after and returned to his previous job at Kodak, leaving my father, in his early teens, to take his place. They planted some alfalfa for their cattle, but mostly used the ground to sow high-moisture ear corn. Although it is a common practice now, my grandfather was said to be the first farmer in the area to realize that if you applied more fertilizer it would lead to more corn. As a result, he achieved some of the highest local yields on the Corps of Engineers' fields.

My grandfather was always one step ahead in farming. He put in one of the first freestall barns and parlors in the region, building most of it himself with the help of a few high school kids. He figured out that feeding grain in the parlor would stimulate more production, as well as milking three times a day instead of two. Both practices became commonplace after he had already adopted them. He made a lot of milk during a time when farming was profitable. He was the type of farmer they put on the cover of agricultural journals.

My grandfather didn't like leaving the house later in life. Once in a while, he would attend a concert or basketball game of mine or my sister's, but that eventually became rarer. When my father and Aunt Kelly were young, my grandparents partied with other farming couples in the area. As a child, my father saw them drink hard and dance in a circle to Hank Williams's "Kaw-Liga," yipping and hollering and pretending to be Native Americans. In the early hours of the morning, they would go to someone's farmhouse and have breakfast before slinking home to milk, if there wasn't a child or hired hand to do it for them. My father told me more than once about the Christmas Eve Grandpa Dennis came back from a party too drunk to do the evening milking. Grandma and my ten-year-old father had to figure out how to milk, even though neither of them had done it before, while my grandfather lay snoring on the couch.

My grandfather came from an era in which success in an occupation defined, in near entirety, who a person was. The details about his life separate from farming are few and hard to collate. He wore polo shirts. He vaguely liked the Yankees. He chewed Wrigley's gum and drank Black Velvet and ginger ale. The only thing he wanted for Christmas was chocolate-covered cherries. I once saw a picture of him in his twenties barrel racing on a quarter horse, but he never spoke about it nor rode a horse after I was born. These facts are hard to stack into anything that gives the impression of a life off the farm.

My grandparents' prefab was next to the pond, so he could have taken up fishing. I would have been happy to fish with him. However, he had no interest in it. He could have gardened or met his siblings in town for coffee. Mostly, instead, he sat in his armchair, watching soapies whose plotlines he had trouble following. It became harder and harder for him to go to summer parades or church breakfasts. Eventually, my grandmother went without him. Before long, the only time he left the house was to go to town to get bananas and put gas in his truck, which he drove around the block twice a day to look at the fields he used to own. When the truck became too difficult for him to drive, he took the Gator instead.

Sometimes my grandfather pulled into a field that my father was working. He parked along the headlands and watched my father chop corn or cut hay for a while. It is tough enough growing old, and worse if it feels like there's nothing left. My grandmother lived for her family, especially her grandchildren. Perhaps my grandfather could have learned to think like that, too, if he didn't have a brain injury. However, the past was recent and would always exist between the three generations of Dennis men. My grandfather had long ago decided that the farm would come first. Now, though, he had nothing to replace it with.

Eventually, my grandfather decided to die.

He was diagnosed with congenital heart failure. As it stood, 35 percent of his heart was inactive. However, the condition could be controlled, if not partly reversed, with healthy eating, exercise, and medication. He could have easily lived another ten years, if not more.

I went to my grandparents with my father to try to get my grandfather to take a walk. Even to the end of the road and back, my father pleaded. My grandfather, however, refused to leave the chair. Instead, he gripped the armrest. My grandmother had gone through thousands of pounds of butter in her lifetime of cooking, and it was not casual for her to attempt anything remotely healthy. Still, understanding the seriousness of my grandfather's heart condition, she made salads, prepared more vegetables, and baked the chicken instead of frying it. Nonetheless, my grandfather pushed the plate away. He had never made dinner for himself, except hot dogs and peanut butter sandwiches the few times my grandmother had traveled. Now, every time she left the house, he got up from his chair to fry sausage, eating more of it than he ever had. Even worse, he quit taking his medication.

Trying to determine the agency of an aging mind is guesswork. He wasn't the man we knew before he hit his head, and his thinking had proven to be anything but clear. A rational person would have taken pills and gone for walks to stay alive. Still, he was always stubborn and wanted to dictate his own conditions. In the end, it didn't matter how much of the old Andy Dennis was left. He had made a decision.

His brothers, Donny and Carlton, showed up at my grandparents' house. They were panicked at hearing about my grandfather's behavior. He was the sibling who was always on top of everything, so it was bewildering to see him sit there with pale skin and a blank stare when it could have been prevented. They accused my grandmother of not looking after him properly. She promised she was doing her best, and given how she too was starting to decline, that was likely true. If there was a time my grandmother could have forced my grandfather to take his medication, it wasn't now, when she started struggling with her memory and speech and relied more on others. Grandma Dennis had a good relationship with my grandfather's brothers, so it was no small thing for them to knock on the door like that. My uncles stood in the living room and begged my grandfather to go to the hospital or some sort of care center. Still, he refused to go.

"I don't want to be alive anymore," he told them.

One day my grandfather wet himself in the chair. I knew this because when I visited, I was told not to sit there. My grandmother had cleaned it, but it was obvious what had happened. Soon after, he stopped getting out of bed. His mind and body grew weaker, fading away, and eventually he stopped speaking. He kept rolling out of the bed, and because my grandmother could not lift him, my father got calls in the middle of the night to pull him off the floor. The local American Legion lent my father a hospital bed with railings on the sides. My father later said that the look in my grandfather's eyes came from a man who regretted dying.

My grandfather's fear of hospitals never left him. Being in that bed seemed to make him think that he had been admitted. He had only lain in it one night when my father, at 11:00 p.m., received one final phone call.

The undertaker came in an hour, but he didn't have any staff with him. He was a slight, older man himself, and not capable of lifting much. Therefore, my father had to carry my grandfather out of the bedroom and into the hearse.

As a boy, he had the same haircut as my grandfather. He played soccer and basketball like my grandfather did, and also drank Miller High Life when he was older. As an adult, Grandpa Dennis was the first person, after my mother, whom he confided in. They saw each other while feeding cows, and then in the fields, and then for a drink together after fieldwork. In these moments, my father would tell him the things he thought or the news he learned. It was obvious to everyone that my father looked up to him. For much of the way, they lived as most fathers and sons hope to be. The two farms were side by side in the same measure that their lives were. My father did what he could to shield my grandfather from the rest of the world after the accident, despite what it cost him. He wanted to protect what was left of my grandfather, because he believed in the person he used to be.

The pastor who did the funeral praised Grandpa Dennis for going out on his own terms, but it was hard for any of us to see it that way. She didn't have to watch him die like my grandmother, my aunt, and my parents did. She didn't have to see that same old stubborn look on his face. No one in our family could rationalize it. To us, it was just one more bad decision at the end of his legacy.

The Aesthetics of Decline

FOR A FEW WEEKS EVERY YEAR, maybe in June or July, the phlox comes in. Their blossoms are purple and white. They line the ditches, the hedge-rows, the sides of buildings, and the edge of woods, filling the valley.

We considered the world hostile to the act of farming. The stretches of rain that kept us out of the field were remembered more than the good weather. The milk market never seemed to be in our favor, the farmgate price getting lower while costs increased. We had the sense that there was always someone behind a desk making money from what we did, even if we couldn't ourselves. Agribusiness still flourished. Retailers made large profits. Farming journals declared the loss of small farms to be natural selection. In total, these truths were the parameters of our livelihood.

Allegany is one of the poorest counties in New York State. It is rural and was made of family farms, but they are mostly gone now. There aren't jobs in Allegany and fewer people are getting an education. People have become angry, but they don't know who to be angry at. Each generation has fewer opportunities and they see themselves further isolated from what they assume to be the rest of the world. Whatever systems govern the country, they know they are at the wrong end of them. Not seeing themselves in national politics, they tend to vote for those who promise to disrupt the status quo, even if they don't have anything to gain from it.

When Earl Butz said that farmers who refused to expand would have to die, he didn't mention that the communities around them would disappear, too. Canaseraga, once a booming railroad town, now barely manages two hundred students in the school, kindergarten through twelfth grade, and will have to close its doors soon. It will follow the bank, the feedstore, and the tractor dealership, which have all left. Their windows are still shuttered. The only businesses that remain are the gas station, a bargain furniture warehouse, and Tom Capwell's small grocery store. Two of the buildings on the town's four corners have already crumbled to rubble.

There are parts of our family's story that are different from others, but that story didn't happen without a context. Very few people knew what my grandfather had done or what my parents went through to keep the farm, because they had their own problems. Still, the decline of the family farm affected all of them. Every time a farm disappeared, it hurt businesses, churches, schools, and organizations in the area. The landscape in America was changing, and what it was turning into didn't have use for most of us.

For two weeks a year, all of this happened between purple and white flowers. It was a strange pairing. What we saw didn't match what we were feeling. It was a type of beauty that almost hurt.

My father told me that if his mind started to go, I should take him to the woods, set him on a log, and shoot him. Because I knew him, I don't think it was entirely in jest. He said it often, and it made me wonder if I had been given a duty. He saw what my grandfather's deterioration did to everyone else and he didn't want to be known that way. I didn't tell many people about my father's request, in case I had to carry it out someday. It would be up to me to make sure it happened on a nice morning with a spot in the woods that had a good view. If I could, I would have wildflowers on the forest floor and have his body caught by the phlox as it fell.

How it all ends seemed like something that would have been within our control, but now we know better. Real stories don't finish in a smoky haze after the final shootout or the band playing the hero's exit. Instead, most people, maybe the strongest ones, keep pushing until they can't push any longer and then that's it. Regardless of our notions or what we told ourselves, the end was coming for us anyway. Last throes are seldom graceful. Already, the things that defined us had rusted and were held together with wire. Driving through Canaseraga, maybe it was obvious that we were all held together with wire.

Where the Milk Goes

THE PARLOR ON OUR FARM WAS BUILT into the old tiestall barn. It was easier than tearing down the original building. The milk had to travel through pipes along the block walls for a considerable distance before entering the milk house and falling into the bulk tank. Despite the hot water and detergent that cleaned the whole system before and after each milking, over time small deposits of milk stone collected at the bottom of the pipes. This raised the bacteria count of the milk that passed over it. When my father milked two hundred cows, the volume was enough that the milk wasn't affected. However, with fewer cows giving less milk, that milk picked up more bacteria along the way. The system wasn't meant to handle the small amount being produced and provided a reasonable explanation for the high bacteria count: bad design.

However, while the quantity of milk making it to the bulk tank had an impact, so did the fact that my father couldn't afford to buy diesel fuel. Often, trying to stretch out days between deliveries, there wasn't enough for the machines we ran. Sometimes my father also didn't have the fuel to put into the hot water heater. Those days the milking system was washed with cold water, which further built up residue.

The bacteria count in the milk was probably close to the limit for a while before finally exceeding it. The milk inspector visited monthly, but this warranted an extra trip. The judgment was left on yellow carbon copy paper. My father was given two weeks to make the required changes and lower the count. In addition to taking down the pipes and cleaning them by hand, he needed to get a new vacuum pump, which he did not have the money for. The inspector probably realized that. When my father had not installed a new vacuum pump after two weeks, he received a phone call from his co-op, Dairy Farmers of America. DFA said that as a penalty they would not pick up his milk for the next two weeks, and would not do so until he installed a new pump.

My father told DFA to fuck themselves.

This marked the second time in his life as a farmer that my father had made that declaration. However, it was different this time. Instead of being exasperated, my father had reached the end. There would be nothing to laugh at later.

Eventually, my father would say that the milk inspector was fair and that he was only guiding our farm towards the inevitable. However, those were the words of a man who had years to consider his past from a philosophical standpoint and to choose how he wanted to think about it. The milk inspector probably was, in fact, an honest man. However, he was part of the system that blocked our farm's income and represented a co-op that was known to have little interest in taking the milk of small farms, despite promising to work on behalf of every farmer.

In the end, after everything my father had gone through to keep farming, he was marked unwanted as a farmer. There were few other co-ops left in the area, and they were small and already at capacity. One said they would look into it and let him know, but they didn't get back to him. For years my father had kept finding ways to make milk, and now, after all of that, there was nowhere to send that milk.

For two weeks, my father unscrewed the bottom of the bulk tank after the morning milking and let the milk flow into the drain, waiting for a phone call that was unlikely to come.

Born a Farmer

As a child, my father had to get the cows before each milking. He woke up early, slipped on his boots, and washed the Surge buckets they used to milk with. Then he walked into the valley while it was still dark in the morning.

The pasture stretched almost to the top of the hill. Later it would be divided into four or five fields of corn and alfalfa, but back then it was all grass. The weeds were bent where he always went over the bank, and where the ground was soft, it held the shape of his boots. There was probably something reassuring in seeing his tracks ahead of him. Two roadways cut through the gulley, and the cows always split in front of them. My father had to push half of the herd through the trees and thick brush and up the bank, and then get back to the top of the other path and move the cattle before the first group turned back. It took him an hour every morning and evening.

An hour is a long time to a child, but it must have been a pleasant walk. He would have been in a field or along the edge of the woods when the sun crested the hill line and shone around him. He would have seen it stir the birds and the gray squirrels that left their nests to caper around the base of trees. The brisk air would feel good before going to school, and getting the cows would give him a chance to have his own thoughts before climbing onto the bus. Then, out there in the evening, he could look back on the day. The summers of his youth had symmetry. Farming must have felt natural then.

My father was popular in high school. He never said it himself, but it was apparent in how his old classmates talked about him and asked what he was up to. My father said that being a farm kid made you cool back then, but there was more to it than that. He had a motorcycle. He dated a lot of women. A lot of people liked him, and I think part of that was because he was friendly to everyone.

My father didn't have much choice in what he did with his life, but that was the way it was back then. Some men were already married or had children coming by the time they graduated high school, and others joined the railroad or electric company a few weeks later and worked there until they retired. They didn't travel in those days. There was no internet to give them ideas about life far away. Instead, there was a local paper that shaped a local world. Without much else to do, they were ready to put on their boots and go to work.

Carlton, Grandpa Dennis's brother, farmed where he, my grandfather, and their siblings grew up. However, he found that he, like my grandfather, couldn't get along with Clair. It might have been their personalities, old issues that sometimes accumulate between parents and their children, or that Clair, having built the barn and being the first Dennis to milk cows, could not tolerate new ideas at his age. After a year of farming, Carlton also found himself in an expensive divorce. He eventually sold the cows and returned to work at Kodak. Soon after, Clair passed away at the age of sixty-five, which was old back then. After Clair's death, the farm was split between all his children. Grandpa Dennis cosigned a loan with my father to pay off his siblings and start a new herd, even though interest rates were at a record high at that time. Circumstances dictated that they went ahead anyway, with both of their names on the mortgage.

My father's first herd had forty-five cows. He started in April 1979, his senior year of high school. Some came from my grandfather's farm, and some he bought himself. He still milked in stainless steel Surge buckets, carrying the milk from each cow to the bulk tank. He fed and milked the cattle before and after classes. Basketball season was already over, and he didn't play baseball.

My grandparents' generation wasn't in an honored war, Korea preferably forgotten. Instead, they grew up in the shadow of the Greatest Generation. It put more pressure on them to uphold and pass down strict ideas of what it meant to be a proper man or woman. Men were to take up the work of their fathers if they were fortunate enough to be born to fathers who had enterprises, and women were to be their wives. Both sexes probably daydreamed of other things, just like my generation did, but they had to keep it to themselves. My father had a life laid out before him and not much choice but to step into it.

For a while, the older generation's vision of life seemed to fit. Farming was good back then. It was a healthy industry. As my father always explained, the harder you worked the more money you made. With that in mind, five years later he doubled his herd to ninety cows.

The postcards of blue skies, green fields, and freshly painted red barns weren't ironic back then. Farmers lived the rural idyll. They carried on a long-standing tradition and got a nod from the rest of the world. They had enough land, capital, and cattle, and banks would help them grow their aspirations. My father enjoyed the independence of having his own farm and making his own decisions, but he also got to partner with my grandfather on the fieldwork. It was a family venture across generations, and that was something to be proud of. It wasn't everyone's perfect America, but it was for people like my father and grandfather.

I wonder if later in life my father thought about getting the cows when he was still a child. He probably longed for a time when he could move without pain, but maybe he went all the way back to when he followed his boot tracks across the gulley. Farmers never talked about nature like other people did because they were used to it. For all that technology has given us, there is something elemental about being human that technology is incapable of speaking to. Farming became more advanced, but it never got better. Instead, the challenges that came next were of a kind that couldn't be solved by working harder. Once he no longer had such undisturbed moments to himself, my father had to find another way to make sense of the world. I wonder if he ever took those long walks again in his mind.

I am sure that if I could go back in time and meet my father after high school, I would recognize him. Other than the tinted glasses and muttonchops he eventually grew out of, he wouldn't have been much different. If I told him what farming would become, he would have listened politely and respectfully like I had seen him do with other people that no one else had time for, but I don't think he would have believed me. There was no reason to prepare for such a future. The only thing I could have done at that point would be to have a beer with him. He wouldn't have drunk gin back then, because he only started doing that after I said that I liked gin. He wouldn't have been a Cubs fan or thought much about zombie movies. In fact, despite all that he would go through the rest of his life, the only way he would change was to care about what the rest of us liked, so we had more to talk about in the milking parlor.

Farming is an occupation built on myths. Some of them seemed true for a while. We were told that the nature of our work made us good people, but then how we did that work changed. We were told that we had to get bigger because we had to feed the world. However, getting bigger is what hurt us all. It was instilled in us that the farm came first before anything else we did, and if we put our back into it, we would be all right. Although we would never be rich, we would gain something more valuable than money. Our place on this earth was to take the farm given to us and pass it on to our sons and daughters, and if we didn't, then we failed. Still, I believe that after everything that had happened to my father, he had found his way to a more honest truth, which was that every farmer had to instead measure for himself what he had done. In the end, there was no redemption or congratulations, and if someone wanted to be proud of what they accomplished, then they had to decide that for themself.

The Way We Go Out

We had two Christmases on the Kramer side. The first one was at Aunt Kim and Uncle David's house with all the extended family the Sunday before the twenty-fifth, and then a smaller gathering at Grandma and Grandpa Kramer's on Christmas Eve. In 2014, Grandpa Kramer decided to throw a "buck party" for the men in the family a few days before the first Christmas. Because Grandma Kramer had no place to go, she was there as well. We ate venison and drank Grandpa Kramer's homemade wine. The wine leaned more on its strength than its taste, and at some point, I drank too much of it. I was explaining to the older generation what I believed to be trends in women's pubic shaving and where my preferences stood. It was only the next day—when my grandmother called and asked if I had urinated on the bathroom mat—that I remembered I did. In fact, the moment came back to me: I had stood in front of the toilet, fell over, and pissed anyway.

I was a bit sheepish at the Sunday Christmas party. My grandmother made it clear that I wasn't forgiven yet. My grandfather, instead, said it was a good time—although no doubt took an earful on my behalf.

Otherwise, the Sunday Kramer Christmas wasn't any different than other years. There was a ham, potatoes, gravy, and lots of desserts. My cousin Josh, having the best sense of humor among us, dressed up as an elf and handed out presents, while another cousin, Kris, played Santa. They gave out small gifts like flashlights and boxes of candy that came from Aunt Edie, and everyone else exchanged sweets or crafts they brought. A photo was taken of Grandpa Kramer and his sisters, all of them coming from Germany more than sixty years earlier. It would become the most circulated picture in our family.

The next day Grandpa Kramer went out to cut firewood. It was a cold and windy day, the kind that would have made most people stay home. My grandfather, however, liked to be in the woods. He collected chainsaws he bought at yard sales and had over twenty of them in his shed. He piled wood not only for his stove, but also for ours, and sometimes for David and Kim. He was extremely easygoing, but he was also very disciplined with himself and believed in work. Despite the weather and being seventy-seven, he went out to cut wood in the morning.

He hadn't come home by the time it got dark in the evening. My grandmother asked David to go to the woods to check on him. There is a field before the small stand of trees my grandfather was cutting. My uncle would have seen that the tire tracks had filled in with snow, and then, in the moonlight reflecting off the field, that my grandfather's truck was still there.

Grandpa Kramer was sitting on a log, slumped. His head hung down. It was an unnatural posture for the man we knew. His glasses were in the snow in front of him. When I came up later with my father and looked at Grandpa Kramer, I realized it might have been the first time that I saw him without his glasses. His face was swollen and blue, and even though he was dead, something inside me still expected him to raise his head with the wide grin he always had.

It appeared that Grandpa Kramer had cut a tree that got tangled in the branches of a second tree and never fell. My grandfather did what you should not do and tried to cut the second tree. He had likely gotten away with it a few times in the past. However, my grandfather was deaf in one ear, and probably didn't hear the cut tree above him turn and fall.

Two days later we gathered for Christmas at his house. We all felt the same way: we didn't want to be there but needed to be. The absence Grandpa Kramer left was large enough already, and then embodied by the empty armchair he always sat in. Because he couldn't hear high-pitched sounds, he never realized that it creaked as he breathed. Once in a while, we caught each other staring at it and its silence. Finally, Grandma Kramer sat in it, which somehow seemed like the right thing to do.

I gave the eulogy for Grandpa Kramer at the small country church nearby. The next day I got on a plane to Iceland with a bad case of diarrhea. I was getting a second master's degree, heading towards a country with little daylight in the winter and expensive alcohol. I did not know how the rest of the family faced the quiet new year ahead, because I was the farthest away.

Meanwhile, it turned cold in western New York. According to my father, it stayed seventeen below zero for two weeks. The parlor is a frigid place, made of blocks and steel and without insulation. He ran an extension cord to an old Salamander heater he carried down the steps, but often didn't have diesel to put into it. Gloves can't be worn while milking because they spread bacteria. Instead, my father's hands were always wet and aching while the parlor rusted in the cold.

Every morning, after milking, my father turned the valve on the bulk tank and emptied the milk into the drain. It pooled and rose up the concrete walls for a few minutes before finally disappearing through the small grate on the floor. Milk is not translucent enough to cast a reflection, but the old halogen bulb in the ceiling threw the shape of my father over the rocking surface. He looked at this pool for two weeks. The milk was hard won, but he didn't have anywhere to send it. He never told anyone what he saw when he stared into the milk.

Grandpa Kramer's death infused the January darkness. He was a larger-than-life presence, and without him in the family everyone felt smaller. It was lonely for my father to go through cold barns to milk and feed rough cattle. My mother worked off the farm during the day. By the time she got back she was tired. Every night they both fell asleep in the shared armchair before 8:00 p.m. I was gone back to a place across the ocean that happened to be Iceland this time but was always somewhere far away. I had been coming and leaving for years now, and my father knew that I couldn't make a life as a modern dairy farmer. Grandpa Dennis had been dead for a while, and the man my father knew him as had been gone before that. Grandpa Kramer often stopped by with a six-pack and shot the shit with my father. My father missed Grandpa Kramer as a friend and maybe as a father figure as well. His death alone wouldn't have caused my father to quit milking cows. He had continued to slip his boots on in the morning for a long time after it was supposed to be possible. However, the loss of Grandpa Kramer was the first major misfortune that occurred separate from the farm. It was the type of tragedy that could happen to anyone in an everyday life, and that was a life my father was supposed to have in addition to farming. My father would later say, "Why die in the barn?" The way one dies was probably still on his mind.

The Last Day a Dennis Milked

MY FATHER WOULD HAVE HAD TROUBLE SLEEPING. He got up early, and probably it was early enough that there were still embers in the woodstove. He would have walked onto the front porch in his wool socks, snow on the concrete melting into the fabric, and taken wood from the pile.

He got a cup of coffee and sat in the armchair. He didn't try to watch TV, because that somehow felt wrong, as if the low voices breaking the silence were disrespectful of the moment. He mostly read crime novels and farm journals, so he would have picked up a Ken Follet or Harlan Coben book, but after a few minutes he left it on the coffee table and sat in the darkness. Eventually he got up and started the milking early.

My father walked to the barn, his breath visible in front of him. His boots scraped the frozen grass, a solitary shadow moving across the lawn. He did his best not to think. His body knew what to do, and only had to do it one more time. It took him across the driveway, underneath the light of a flickering dust-to-dawn bulb on the electric pole, and into the milk house.

He had to run the hose to fill the sink with wash water that would clean the milkers. I don't know if he realized that it didn't matter if the milkers were washed, because the milk was going to be dumped and the cows sent away. I do know, however, that he would have set the system to wash regardless, watching the sink fill up.

Some of the cows rose to their feet once they saw my father. He did not call them beautiful bitches this time, nor any other name. A few of them might be taken home from the weekly auction by another dairy farmer who would milk them, but most would be bought as beef. He had to call today to see when the hauler was coming. The only light still working in the rafters bleached the cows pale. My father stared ahead as he tapped the stalls and headed them towards the parlor.

There is a time between putting the milkers on a row of cows and taking them off that a man has a chance to think. These were the worst moments for my father. There is the temptation to see him looking back through all the years of milking with nostalgia, revisiting the changes that have occurred and how he had changed with them. If he were a character in a book or movie, then that might be true. Instead, I believe the moment was too heavy and too hard for him to do that. I imagine that he paced the pit back and forth, his boots rubbing against the rubber mat on the floor. Or, when I really think about it, I see him sitting on an overturned bucket with his head in his hands.

There was no one to talk to in the parlor. Even if he knew what he was feeling, there was no one to tell it to. The beating pulse of the milkers around him would soon go still, and that would be a type of silence he had never faced before. He didn't yell at the cows when he herded them into the parlor. Maybe he rubbed the necks of a few of them. Maybe he stood on the top of the steps and watched their breath billow out in the holding area. They weren't the registered Holsteins of his tiestall herd, and they were gangly and battered like most freestall cattle, but he knew them. Once the trailer jolted down the driveway with the last load, there would be an emptiness on the farm that would remain as long as there were Dennises there. By now, the barn cats started to collect around the door of the parlor, sensing the end of the milking. What my father poured into their dish would be the last milk they would ever drink. Like the rest of us, they would have to find a way to survive in the world without it.

When the cows were all milked, my father set the milkers to wash. He scraped, and then hosed down the parlor. He turned the lights off, and then the radio. Then there was only the throbbing of the milkers as the chlorinated water heaved through them. He went to the milk house and rinsed the weathered floor, pushing away any chaff he might have tracked in. I think he teared up at this point. He might have held it in through the whole milking, but by now he was pressing his fingers into his eyes without making any sound.

Then the wash cycle stopped, and when the pulsation ended, so did a history. He walked away without turning back. There would be time one day for introspection. Right now, he just needed to make a phone call.

The Machinery Sale

THE SOUNDS OF VEHICLE DOORS SHUTTING punctuated the murmur. Trucks lined the road to the top of both hills, half in the ditch. People collected together in our lawn, standing with their arms folded, looking around for someone to talk to until the auction started. Because it was the first sale of the spring, it brought a good crowd, even if most people had no intention of buying our equipment. Some wanted a sense of what machinery was going for that year. Some wanted to pass the time. No one discussed the absurdity of farming, because it was already around them.

Neighbors and family members came as well, which gave it the feeling of a funeral. There wasn't much they could do to help out, nor was there anything they could say to my father. Most people gave him a polite nod as he passed by and allowed him his space.

Years later, my father said what we could have guessed anyway, which was that there's a sense of failure when someone sells their cows. I asked him how long he felt like that. He thought about it for a while, and then said two years. I don't know if the length of the feeling was specific or not. I only know when it started.

Hot dogs, hamburgers, and cake were set out on the porch. There were no decorations, however, nor banners from companies. No one shook anyone's hand.

There are stories of farmers who stayed in the house while their equipment was auctioned off. No one blamed them. As hard as it was for my father to stand in front of the public and watch his tractors and implements go, however, he wasn't the type to shy away from it. He would see out the dismantling of his farm. The auctioneer had done many sales before and knew how to keep my father busy, having him start the tractors before the bidding and answer questions about the machinery.

All our equipment had been pulled into the lawn and onto the bank next to the driveway. Most of it had been wiped down with an old T-shirt. People milled in the spaces between the machinery, checking that the tongues weren't bent, or whether the grease fittings were rusted or not to get a sense of how well the implement had been taken care of. Occasionally, someone lifted a hood and started an engine to listen to it. If something needed to be replaced, it would be mentioned in the sales book or at the start of the bidding, but anyone interested would look for themself. The haybine and baler were in good shape, even if they were older models than what most dairy farmers had. The Ford 8870, our biggest tractor, had little braking due to a manufacturing flaw. For years we just used the parking brake. The John Deere 4455 needed an engine overhaul. The mixer wagon was battered by age, and few farmers used the type of silage wagons we did. People walked around these machines with catalogues rolled in their back pockets. They made a judgment on each numbered lot, but also got a sense of the story they told.

Before my father quit, milk had been high for a week. Because of that, the price of cattle had a chance at being better than it had been, and it could be a while before a similar opportunity came again. The first call my father made was to see if the large operation that bought my grandfather's farm would also rent my father's land. The next call was to a hauler to pick up his cows.

Because my father didn't use a computer back then, it would have been my mother who sent the email. I was in my dorm room in Iceland when almost one hundred years of dairy farming in the Dennis family came to an end. It was delivered in two lines:

> We wanted to tell you before you heard it from someone else:
> we sold the cows. Call when you want.

After I clicked on the phone icon in Skype, there was a pause before it started ringing, and in that time I had to keep myself from hanging up. Iceland is five hours ahead of New York in the winter, so it was nearly 11:00 a.m. before I could call. The sun had just risen over the horizon with its amber light and would set again in a couple of hours.

"How's it going over there?" my father asked, after he picked up.

Because he said it in a good-natured way, it was disarming and I had to resist the temptation to answer him. There was silence in my room, except for the sound of distant traffic coming through the closed window. In the background my mother cleared her throat, likely without realizing it. I knew their dog passed by because I could hear its toenails on the kitchen linoleum. "You should have told me first," I said.

My father started to speak but I cut him off.

"Didn't I work next to you all those years without getting anything from it? Aren't I at least owed to know you're going to quit before you do it?" Suddenly, I was a kid again, the one who couldn't sit in on the loan meetings in the kitchen or that saw the adults stop talking about the business of farming whenever he entered the room. I started crying.

It took me a while, maybe years, to realize the guts my father needed to stop milking cows. On paper, it was inevitable. The farm was in a hole that it could never get out of, and farming was never going to be possible again for a herd of that size. To carry on each day was hard, harder than I still probably realize, and the self-made miracles had run out. Now, looking back, I can understand better why he didn't discuss his decision. It took all he had to make those two phone calls, and to have anyone telling him not to or ask him to think it through again could have made him lose his nerve. He couldn't afford to hesitate. Ultimately, not to die in a barn takes courage.

The machinery didn't bring as much as he hoped. Before the sale, he owed the Farm Service Agency $200,000, and at the end of the day he was still $16,000 short. FSA would let him pay it off gradually, but it would have to come out of whatever my parents did next.

For my father's entire life, everything in front of him had been certain. When he was a child, he had chores, and then he had to milk his father's cows. Before long, he had his own cows to milk. He milked and fed regardless of whatever else went on in the world, farming where he stood for thirty-seven years. His hands and body had the memory of all that work in them. Now, suddenly, he didn't have the milking and feeding and fieldwork to tell him who he was. All that was in front of him was a crowd of people avoiding his eyes.

It would have been better if, having made it through the sale, all his equipment would have been gone before sunset. The next morning, my parents could have rubbed their faces and started moving on. However, many buyers had to find someone to haul what they had bought or come back with a tractor themselves to take it to their own place. A lot of equipment was still left the following day, and some farmers didn't return for a week or two. The 4455, silage wagon, and plow sitting in the grass of the bank made it easier to remember the auction and what it meant. Every day my father stared outside the kitchen window at the tractors that were no longer his.

The haybine was the last to be picked up.

No One Said What Farming Was

I TURNED TO MY FATHER. "Why don't farmers protest?"

We were riding in the tractor as he fed the cows. The chute of the TMR mixer discharged silage in pulses that fell to the bunk silently. I don't know what age I was, but I was in high school. The cows crowded in front of the machine and tossed their heads when silage fell over them. My father mumbled about there being some isolated examples in the past, but then said that American farmers were probably groomed to be too competitive with each other. They were told that they had to keep getting larger than their neighbor because the pie was only so big, and because of that they never learned to cooperate. After one side of the barn had been fed, he drove out of the building and turned around in the driveway. We rocked back and forth in unison as the tractor rolled across old ruts. Because the space in the cab was limited, I had to keep my knees together and shoved against the side to make sure my legs didn't touch his. I asked my father the same question again.

He sighed. "Probably the best a farmer can do is to take care of his own corner. Be a good steward with what he has."

"That's bullshit," I said.

One of the most frustrating aspects of dairy farming back then was not knowing who to blame. Family farmers struggled and it felt obvious that there were unethical forces out there. However, as far as anyone knew, they didn't have a face. When I asked other farmers about it, they mentioned the low milk price and high cost of feed, but couldn't tell me anything that seemed like they figured out how it all went wrong. Few of us had little more than a vague idea of how milk was priced. Since the nineties, milk was divided into four classes based on how it was

consumed—fluid, soft products, hard cheese, and powdered milk—
and given different prices accordingly. We were told the cheese price
mattered the most and that it was traded on the Chicago Mercantile
Exchange. How it was all calculated into the monthly farmgate price,
however, no one could explain. We just knew that the milk price was too
low more times than not. Different pricing systems evolved, and farmers
knew the terms and buzzwords associated with them, but it was still a
dark magic we had no control over.

In the tractor, I told my father that it should be the goal of every
person to change the world, and although ninety-nine out of a hundred
people are going to end up looking foolish, sometimes someone makes
a difference. Teenagers are prone to righteous anger. My father nodded
and said okay. That angered me more and I said that the current system
of doing nothing wasn't really working well, so what did he know?

I contacted more than fifty dairy professors, economists, editors of
agricultural journals, and other figures who had a knowledgeable role in
the dairy industry. The internet was still young back then, and the fact
that I could find the phone numbers for all these people seemed further
proof that I should call them. The aim was to put a name or date to the
thing that stood against families like mine. I asked them all one question: Why are family farms struggling?

The dairy sector in America is extremely volatile, prices going up
and down dramatically, sometimes within weeks. At the moment I
placed those calls, however, the milk price was apparently sufficient.
Nearly every industry leader that I talked with said that family farms
weren't struggling. Farming was fine, they asserted, and the system
wasn't broken. A syndicated reporter on milk markets, one that many
farmers got their information from, said what they were all thinking:
he didn't like Walmart coming in and putting mom-and-pop stores
out of business, but there was nothing to do to stop it. It was simple
economics. In the same way, it was a shame that some family farms

were going out of business because they couldn't compete, but it was altogether inevitable.

Of approximately fifty people who were meant to understand the logistics of the dairy industry in America, only two of them agreed that it had problems. Dr. Ron Cotterill of the University of Connecticut was working on a new way to calculate farmgate prices that balanced profits more fairly between farmers and retailers. He would try for years to get the bill adopted by the Connecticut State Legislature, but never succeed. Dr. Richard A. Levins from the University of Minnesota wrote a book that chronicled the life of his friend and colleague Willard Cochrane, an economic advisor to President Kennedy who foresaw the problems with expansionist agriculture before anyone else. It tells how Cochrane tried to save family farming through supply control, but was eventually called a communist and run out of Washington.

I was young and naive, thinking that I could figure out the flaws of the dairy industry. To make it worse, it was a time when only farmers themselves believed these problems existed. I was left feeling foolish. The next time I rode with my father while he fed, I was silent, staring out the window at the silage flung at cows. Now, those forty-eight people, and all those like them who have steered the industry since then, are shaking their heads at the end of family farming, lamenting how no one could have seen it coming.

A Happy Story

We COULD HEAR A VEHICLE SLOWING on the dirt road before it appeared at the gate and turned in. The first relatives coasted under the locust trees and parked next to our truck. If they had a dog, that dog leapt out of the back first, darted to the pavilion to sniff us, and then ran to the water. Eventually a small pack of border collies chased each other around the bank and barked at the children in the pond. The same singsong hello was repeated each time someone arrived. The picnic table filled with salt potatoes, potato salad, baked beans, chocolate chip cookies, and bags of Lay's. Everyone brought the type of beer they drank, and sometimes, as a gesture, the type of beer someone else drank. Usually, my father went up an hour early to get the fire started. If I was there, we would drink a Miller High Life and watch the diesel burn off the wood.

We used copper sulfate to kill the weeds once a year, keeping the water clean for swimming, and dyed the pond to stop the algae from growing. We mowed the lawn every week because if it got too long and then was cut, it would leave brown spots. Starting with blue water and green grass made all other details smaller. We stained the pavilion and painted the dock when it was needed. We put sand where people got in and out of the pond. Every handful of years we trimmed the juniper bush. Keeping the pond nice was something we could do, and was probably more for us than the people who visited.

Once the fire was going my parents spread plastic chairs around the edge of the pavilion. When someone sat down someone else asked them if they wanted a beer, and then said to go ahead and take one of theirs from the cooler. Sometimes someone would pick on someone else for drinking a "water beer," which was what Grandpa Kramer had called domestic lagers. Grandma Kramer would say wasn't it cold this week or wasn't it hot, and everyone would agree. My father kept an eye on the fire. When it settled to coals, he took unhusked ears of corn from a pail of water and put them on the grill.

When I was small, horseshoe stakes were set up in the lawn, but for most of my life we brought out a basketball, football, Wiffle ball, bat, Frisbee, and whatever else we had and left them in the grass. For a while, we had a pitching wedge and used golf balls Grandma Kramer had found at a yard sale. Before we ate, Jeff and Kelly usually tossed a football or played horse with me, my sister, and their daughters. Uncle David and my father would tell each other about something they tried to fix on the farm or in the house, and whether or not it worked. At first most conversations would be near the food under the pavilion, but then eventually people broke off to sit by the fire or under the shade of the Japanese maple, depending on the weather. The small children would stay in the pond most of the time and only leave when dragged out in tears. The adults jumped in themselves once or twice.

In trying to tell our story I asked my family about their parts in it, but I asked my father the most. When he looked back on his life he tried to be kind to the people in it. The last years he farmed brought him into conflict with a handful of individuals, which was rare for a man people always liked. Maybe it was because he knew I might write about it some-day, or maybe he thought it better to live without resentment as much as was in his power. Either way, he described the milkman, the M&T bank manager, the milk inspector, and others like them as someone doing their job. The system was broken, he said, but they weren't the people who made it. Sometimes my father spoke of my grandfather with anger over what he had done to him, but more often, and more so over the years, it was with the consideration of a man who stepped outside of his past and decided what to take from it. My father knew better than any-one else how difficult it was not to become the injuries life has given you.

In the end, the story of our family is partly shared with other families who struggled to farm at the same time. We can't divest it from the economic conditions that were out of our control and affected everyone, because we lived those changes. However, in the same way, we can't let them speak for everything. It was also the choices we made and how we handled them, and maybe more importantly, how we thought of ourselves afterwards. My father was generous in giving his understanding of it all. He only asked one thing from me in exchange, and that was to make it a happy story.

When there was a lull in the conversation, my father got up and walked around the water. Early in the summer, the juvenile bass lined the shore, suspended in inanimation until he got close enough and they scurried into the algae. Later, the bluegills circled over their nests, the light tip of their dorsal fins slowly undulating. On hotter days, water skippers bunched and flecked the surface, causing the sunshine to sparkle. The floating eyes of bullfrogs watched him pass. More times than not my father stopped at the far end of the pond and looked out, the weeds of the bank swaying below him.

My father pointed out that we got to keep the land, the 450 acres that remained after Grandpa Dennis's death. It was the original ground that Clair had farmed on. Clair was gone long before I was born, so I don't know the type of person he was or what he would have thought of us. I lived in the house that he did and fed calves in the barn he built, but we inhabited different times. To be swimming in the pond generations after Clair dug it for his cattle suggests that some things come full circle. However, the fact that the same farm ended puts a different geometry on everything. There was pain that came in different ways, and it took something from us. Some days were hard. Still, I believe we found reasons to make it a happy story, and they were mostly in each other.

Any given Sunday, most people in our family took a moment to stand on the bank of our pond and look down the hill. Below was our family's history. I took my turn to look, too. In those hedgerows were rocks put there by Dennises through the years, and handkerchiefs and old shotgun shells and other ways we bared parts of ourselves there. Still farther is our silo and the top of our barn. This is the farthest we can see it from. They have taken down my grandfather's silo and sold it for scrap, but we know where it was. There are wet spots that some seasons I got stuck in and other years avoided. Other fields hold other memories. My youth stretched among them all. The fields of the valley below me have names that we have given them, and I am the last keeper of those names. I haven't traced their headlands with tractor tires as many times as the men that came before me, but I was on them long enough to know their shape and to be shaped by them. The ground has rusting bolts and plow parts and Wrigley gum wrappers that we left behind. They will be part of the story the ground tells after us, until all these things, like our own bones, sink into the bedrock and join the Earth's past.

The sun grew a shade deeper as it headed towards the late afternoon. Everyone used to pack up their coolers before four o'clock to milk and do calf chores. Uncle David sold his cows a few years after my father, leaving only Kelly and Jeff with dairy cattle. Still, even if there was nothing that most of us had to do anymore, the old rhythms died hard, and people mostly dispersed. Sometimes, after everyone else was gone, my father would fish with me for a while or take a book out of the truck and read. Eventually, before dinnertime, my parents, my sister, and I put the chairs back in the shed and lifted the cooler into the back of the pickup. Then we got in the truck and went down the hill. The fire was left to burn itself out, cinders still pulsing as evening fell and the bullfrogs started croaking.

The End

T HE PROBLEM WITH STORIES is that if you don't finish telling them, the ending will eventually change. On November 16, 2021, I once again received an email to call home. Part of me knew what it was about before my mother picked up.

My father hadn't slept the night before. He had been driving a school bus for seven years after selling the dairy cattle. He went on his morning route, but then told his coworkers that he felt ill. He left work early, which he had never done before. When he did not return for his afternoon run his co-workers called him, but he didn't answer. One of them went to our farm to look for him, but didn't see him anywhere. She called my mother. My mother immediately left work and came home. After walking around the corner of the shed she found my father slumped over the steering wheel of the tractor.

I already had a plane ticket for the last week in November. It was going to be my first chance to spend Thanksgiving with my family in over fifteen years. The last time I talked with my father, he had gotten the dates wrong and thought I was arriving on the eighteenth. In the end, he was right. I came home on November 18, but my father wasn't there.

The next morning, Uncle David started our Massey Ferguson and put a round bale into my father's beef cows. I watched him from the kitchen window. Then I put on my hat and boots.

He pulled the parking brake as soon as he saw me and walked the rest of the way up the driveway. He stared at the ground until he was in front of me. His eyes were red and watery. He hugged me, the fabric of our winter coats pressed between us.

"I didn't know you'd be home this quick," he said. "I wanted to do something, but I didn't know what to do." He unzipped his jacket and took out an envelope. "You know I'm not good with words."

He handed it to me. I folded it in two and put it in my front pocket. He said that he didn't mind feeding the beef, and that it was up to me if I wanted to take it over. I told him I would.

Later that day I opened the letter. It said that my uncle felt that he owed it to my father to write something to me, and that he never knew a man so strong and easygoing. It talked about what it meant for a son to lose his dad and how life was then different. It said that he was sorry that I had to find that out. My uncle loved my father like a brother and missed him, and he would help with the cattle. My uncle wasn't a person who wrote letters, and it took a lot for him to write this one.

At the funeral, I gave the eulogy and talked about a man who told himself to rock 'n' roll. Some people had to stand along the walls and in the aisle because the church was too full. The door was kept open for those on the steps. I spoke about the yellow model airplane that we watched disappear the first time we flew it because it was a story my father often told. I said that my father was a man of stories, that he could look at the same life that the rest of us were living, too, and find in it something amusing, something to smile about. I told everyone there that my father was the type of person who other people wanted to be around, and although that sounds like a simple thing, the vitality he brought to a group was special. I said that he had courage to reinvent himself and start a new career at fifty-three. I described him as tough and resilient, and insisted that those words fit not because he could still live through everything that he experienced, but because he still enjoyed that life.

Before, I thought that a funeral was a grand summation of a person, but it isn't. Those who love someone who is gone are in too much pain to get the words right. I couldn't do my father justice. After the service, more people shook our hands and then we went to the dinner put on by the American Legion. When it was all over, we went home to a quiet house.

My mother asked me to send in the cattle before I went back to Ireland. I didn't do it right away. Instead, when I got up in the morning, I put my boots on and walked across the lawn. The snow crunched under my feet, because it was the time of year that it would melt and refreeze. I started the tractor and sat on it long enough for it to warm up. I breathed in the exhaust that swelled under the lean-to roof. I tried not to think, especially that sitting on that tractor, on that spot, was the last thing my father did alive. Then I put it into gear. I stabbed the Massey's fork into the first round bale in a row by the driveway and drove it towards the pasture.

I unhooked the gate and tossed the handle into the frosted grass. Sometimes the electricity in it ticked if it was touching a stone. The wire always looped and tangled over itself. I drove the tractor between leaning fence posts, slowly. Because the tractor went over the same ruts every day, the ground was muddy no matter how cold it got. The Massey was a small model, so I pushed the throttle through the worst spots and didn't stop, even if there were cattle in front of me. When I got to the knoll in the pasture, near the round bale ring, I pulled the brake. Cows lingered around the tires, their colors dulled by winter dirt. I swiped at the frozen crust on the bale with an old jackknife, over and over again, until it cut the nylon twine. When I pulled the twine away, I balled it up and left it on the floor of the Massey. Then I drove towards the ring. Once the bale was over it, I tipped the bucket until the bale slipped in.

I sat on the tractor, at the top of the pasture, and cried. I cried since I was feeding cows because my father was no longer there, and I would never see him again. I would never hear him tell a story or ride with him to town. He wasn't going to be at the airport the next time I came home. I cried because no matter how we chose what to take from everything that happened to us, this was how it all finished. His death was too soon. For as hard as he worked, he never got the chance to retire and enjoy time for himself. I cried, because when those ragtag beef cows were not there, then some last part of him would be gone, too. He was another person who waited for me until he couldn't wait any longer.

The decision of whether to stay on the farm was heavy on me in my youth. The consequences were not only mine. There, in the cold pasture and the long winter that followed, that question was replaced by a similar one: Did I do right by my father? It finds me in quiet moments, settling into other thoughts and leaning me towards it. I don't ask other people because they would say what they ought to, which is that there's no sense feeling ashamed because it couldn't have gone any other way. However, the fact that I have to think for myself is a lesson that came hard, but one that I hold on to.

At first, I thought the work in front of me was to forgive my grandfather. Maybe part of it is, and I probably owe that to my father. The best way to honor him might be to picture the three of us in a field: working the ground in a late spring haze, a still image of Dennis men farming together. My father will plow, I will disk, and my grandfather will seed corn or timothy. We'll wave to each other as we pass, the sounds of the other tractors coming through our windows muted. The three generations turning around each other will have meant that something was fulfilled. Then I'll let it all move into the glare of a low sun and give one final comment of a day's work being finished.

The hard labor, financial struggle, and danger of working with animals and machinery is the known part of farming. What's rarely discussed are the stakes for the people who do it. Their identity is on the line every time they get up to milk cows and wait for the next milk check. Everyone in our family, in relationship to the farm, carried some sort of burden. My father said he should have handled my grandfather's decline differently. My mother wished she had gone out to the barn earlier the day my father got hurt. Aunt Kelly always wondered if she should have left her parents' farm or tried to take it over herself, as did my sister on the farm we grew up on. Everyone walked away with their own ghosts. For those growing up on a farm, that farm is a center of gravity, and when someone is so invested in something, there's a pull on them when it doesn't work out.

Now that I don't have either, the farm and my father have become feelings that have merged in my chest. I bring them with me to the cities I move to and the people I meet, and to the streets that are very different from the fields I had known. They're there in how I see the world and in the expressions I give when I think no one is looking. I'm never in a moment and place on its own anymore. This is what I know now: that when the rhythms of farming stop, they become a sentiment that takes over a person. I join a dazed generation of farmers' children looking for ways to move past the guilt. Even if I understand that some-day, when I think of my father and the farm we lived on, it should be only good memories.

In the end, that's something owed to every person who had a farm. They gave of themselves in a way that wasn't given back by the times they lived in. Empty barns and old silos are the only monuments bear-ing their memory, and they require interpretation. When family farm-ing disappeared, it was all of our loss. One of the reasons that no one talks about agriculture anymore is because they don't like what it has turned into. We owe it to those families to recognize that what they went through wasn't inevitable, but a way in which they were failed by others.

If I could, I would ask for one more time with my father in the parlor or the tractor. I wouldn't care what we talked about. He could tell me the whole plot of a movie I haven't seen yet, even if it ruins it. He could tell me a story from his high school days that I had already heard over and over. I just want to see him laugh again, because that was what he did no matter how much pain he was in or what happened on the farm. Sometimes when we were in the truck or the tractor cab, he would tell me that I was quiet. It was in jest, because that was how he knew me to be. If I could sit next to him on the armrest once more, I wouldn't be so quiet this time. We could talk about the Cubs and the Bills, and then in the next silence I would tell him how incredible it was what he came through, and that I was proud to be his son.

I would tell him that I loved him.

Losing Champ

My mother bought a plastic helicopter at a yard sale for twenty-five cents. It was remote controlled but difficult to maneuver and the battery only lasted two minutes. Still, every day, my father tried to fly it. The cheap toy took off in a crooked path and quickly crashed into the dog or the legs of the kitchen table. The sight of a man in his fifties refusing to put down a child's plaything produced mixed conclusions in the household.

From the motivation somewhere between finding a good Christmas present and allowing my father to redeem his childhood, I bought him a model airplane. Bright yellow and sturdily built, it was a Champ RTF—and although a beginner's model, nevertheless the real deal. The box had a young teenage boy in a checkered jumper holding it up and smiling. The kid was irrefutably happy. This, I knew, was the plane for my father.

He wanted to wait until summer when I was home to fly it for the first time. I read the directions and learned how to charge the batteries. The lever went one way to steer it up and down and another to direct it right or left. A second stick controlled the speed. After the first flight, the adjustments would have to be "trimmed" to make sure the controls flew the plane straight. I laughed at the bolded letters inside the manual that read, "If you panic or lose control during the flight drop the hand-held remote."

One summer evening, after chores, we took the Champ RTF to the top of the hill. The field was forty acres across, and beyond that were woods and another valley. We leaned an old two-by-four on a cement block that would be the runway for the plane's maiden voyage. I handed the controls to my father. He waved me off, as was his habit of showing restraint when he was most excited. "You can have the first one," he said. I was reluctant to agree because it was his gift, but knew there was no point arguing.

The little yellow plane accelerated up the board and took off over the first cutting with a tinny buzz. It gained altitude fast and soared over the open land as smoothly as any commercial flight, its silhouette moving across the hay in the last of the sun. Since the adjustments weren't trimmed yet, however, it spun in a circle as it rose.

"Cool tricks," my father said.

I gave a nervous laugh.

I tried to adjust the wings like the manual said, but it seemed to have no effect. The plane continued to twist, and without my direction, climb higher.

"Wow, it can fly pretty far," my father said.

I jammed the control lever one way, trying to curve the plane back towards us, and when that did nothing, jammed it the other way. I pressed the trim buttons on one side and then frantically on the other. I tapped on the batteries in the back. The plane kept turning, higher and farther away from us.

"You should probably bring it back now," my father said.

"I'm trying," I said.

"Bring it back now," he said.

"I can't!"

He grabbed the controls and pushed down on the levers. The plane was nearing the trees. He slammed the controls against his palm, wildly pressing buttons, and then thrust it back in my hands.

I did the only thing I could think of: I dropped the controls in the grass.

The Champ RTF circled through the summer night, slowly, methodically. The distance between us grew, until it was over the forest and then only a small, spinning shadow. Eventually, there was no way to tell it apart from a real airplane miles away or a bird drifting through the air. And then, as we stood there, it disappeared for good.

My father and I jumped into the pickup and coasted down the roads behind the woods, but admitted that it would take too much luck to find it in the ditch. I walked through the forest, but since it was already dark, I would have missed the crash site if I passed by it. My father talked to the old man who owned the Christmas tree lot nearby, and he promised to keep an eye out for it. My father even called Uncle David, who lived a mile down the valley, and asked—jokingly, but perhaps with some desperation—if there was a little yellow plane flying over his house. For weeks afterwards, in silent moments, my father would turn to me and say out loud what he was thinking, which was always "Champ is gone, isn't he?"

"Yes," I would say. "Champ is gone."

We never figured out what happened. Maybe the plane had flown out of range of the receiver. Maybe the controls were broken. It might have been, and I gulp at the thought, operator error. The other part of the story is this: because it was only a toy airplane, we laughed about it for a long time. There was a moment of stunned silence as it disappeared out of view, and then we roared the hardest we had all summer. For days, the very thought of it would crack us up. It became a long-standing joke. My father and I had something more to share between us, another thread connecting us in the time we had together. Champ went from being a model airplane to being a memory between a father and a son. Maybe that is the best fate for all things in life.

Appendix

Twelve Moments That Killed the American Family Dairy Farm

As a child, I liked hearing farmers talk. It was the best part of going to shows, sales, or the feed store. There exchanges were in a language that was hard-earned, and any humility was never entirely coy because of the nature of farming itself. A quiet probing underlay the banter and common jokes, as if everyone was looking for a sign of how the other person's farm was doing, even if that was information that would never be given. They would ask how the hay was going or if they got their corn in, and if they could, they would complain about the weather. Ultimately, in these brief conversations, what they were really saying was, "We're still here, somehow."

By the time I got older, there was a resignation in the way farmers spoke. It was subtle, in how someone shrugged their shoulders before smiling, or repeated, "What can you do?" once too often. Whoever could read these gestures knew that people were starting to worry. The farmgate price had always been volatile, but the highs weren't compensating lows like they used to, and it made farming precarious. As it got harder, the comments about not making money had less humor behind them.

Eventually, as farms went out of business, the conversations changed. Some older farmers may have been fortunate, able to hold on long enough to sell to someone expanding and then call it retiring. "These big outfits," they'd say. "It's not my type of farming. It's the only way to make it, though." The luckiest farmers benefited from one of the three G's: gravel, gas, or Grandma's money. Mineral rights, land that could be quarried, or in some cases, windmill contracts provided extra income that made farming more possible, but even that didn't sustain many farms for long. Farmers who grew bigger suddenly explained what they did with more businesslike language, which was probably more appropriate to the managerial role they now had.

Most farmers felt like the system was against them. They knew that something bigger than themselves was controlling things. Every once in a while, there were rumors of milk coming in from the Canadian border or that Kraft was manipulating the market to lower the milk price. They felt Monsanto tightening its grip with the seed that farmers bought and tractor companies making it harder for them to repair their own equipment. Still, in all the talk among farmers that I was party to, no one ever pinned down why family farms had to struggle. None of them could put a face or a name to whatever stood against them. Without getting at least that far, small farmers were left with no choice but to see themselves as a species that had run its course.

The major events that deterred family farming have been called "moments" here, but that is sometimes a misnomer. Often, the impetus for the outcomes described below had built up for years before the specific date given on this list, and the act itself was the culmination of a certain momentum. Nonetheless, I hope it is a start at assigning responsibility. It is worth saying again clearly: The loss of the family dairy farm in America was not inevitable. It could have been prevented. Instead, it was the consequence of decisions by specific individuals and organizations, often in the pursuit of their own gain.

It's sometimes pointed out that most large farms are also owned by families—usually multiple families, and therefore some may dispute the way I define the term "family farm." In fact, most operations, regardless of their size, likely consider themselves family farms. However, I believe the designation is worth fighting for. I would argue that consumers and those who farm in a way that is better for animals, communities, and the environment agree about what those words mean. A specific group of people paid a price for that description, and because of that, large farming should not have access to it.

Finally, economics, far from being a pure science, is highly politicized. Some might disagree with the claims below or have better ideas to offer. If that disagreement leads to discussion, it means that people are still talking about family farming, and such conversation should continue. Of my reasons for making this list, the first is for my teenage self. I want to try to give him the answer that no one else could, even if it isn't perfect. He's owed at least that much.

At times, I was tempted to see this memoir as a eulogy project. Most family farms have disappeared in the United States. To save those that remain is going to take a significant shift from the type of thinking that got us here, and time is short. To forfeit the American dairy industry entirely to factory production, however, is to turn our backs on not just the small farms that still persist, but also those throughout history who have resisted that understanding of agriculture as long as they could.

There are reasons to be hopeful. A push for supply management exists in a way that hasn't been present in the United States for decades. While putting a quota on the amount of milk that a farmer can produce has its drawbacks, countries such as Canada and Iceland have used it to successfully sustain small farming. Groups like Dairy Together are gathering support for the type of change that slows runaway expansion, and the National Farmers Union continues to work towards legislation that benefits family farms.

The other reason to believe that something good can still happen is that the public has never abandoned the American family farm. People are more concerned than ever about where their food comes from, often asserting that they would pay more for a gallon of milk if the proceeds went to the farmer. Both the consumer and the farmer want cows to be happy and on pasture. What has arguably never happened in the United States, however, is a large-scale and significant way for consumers to support family farms. The farm organizations mentioned above need a bridge to consumers so that public goodwill can turn into action. There must be a way for the average person to help small farms, because small farms need to be paid more for what they do, even if the path toward accomplishing that is not simple. Whatever the approach may be, it will involve restructuring agricultural policy, our food system, and maybe even the way we think about milk. However, to back smaller farming is to acknowledge how these families sustain rural communities, produce a better product, and allow us to celebrate the type of agriculture that occurs in the United States. To change the American dairy industry is going to take something big, and we all need to be in on it.

Understanding how the American dairy industry reached its current state, however, can inform the act of moving forward. Here's one person's suggestion of how family farming became unviable. For the sake of farmers everywhere, let's hope we have learned something.

November 12, 1919
The Founding of Farm Bureau

The American Farm Bureau Federation was founded to counter other associations that represented small farmers at the time, and it increased its reach during the New Deal era under Roosevelt. The organization was crucial in promoting the Agricultural Adjustment Act of 1933 that sought to reduce supply surpluses, and although not a governmental organization, was permitted to take over management of the program once the law was enacted. This essentially allowed Farm Bureau to use government resources to expand its county and state structures. As a result, its membership and influence grew quickly.

Farm Bureau immediately began to push for policies that favored large farms while opposing more progressive legislation, and since then has built close ties with agribusiness. Recent examples include working to remove supply-control measures and encourage greater production with the 1996 farm bill. This led to overproduction and lower farmgate prices, which hurt farmers but benefited agribusiness companies. In

2006, the organization joined with Cargill, Dow Chemical, and other multinationals to promote free trade agreements, some of which eventually caused many US agricultural sectors to be overwhelmed by cheaper imports. From 2002 to 2008, it went against the will of beef producers by siding with corporate meatpackers in fighting against country of origin labeling (COOL) before reversing course in 2008. In 2010, the USDA and US Department of Justice held a joint investigation into the concentration of agricultural markets, as in most sectors only one or several agribusiness companies control a majority of the market. Farm Bureau was notably absent from the hearings. In 2017, it opposed other farm organizations on reforms that would benefit farmers in the proposed Cattle Price Discovery and Transparency Act. Today, Farm Bureau continues to fight climate-related action and other regulations on large farms, often at the expense of small producers.

With an emphasis on representing family farmers, the National Farmers Union stands as the most significant counterpart to Farm Bureau. Predating Farm Bureau, NFU often clashes with the larger organization, particularly in its focus on reducing the influence of corporate agriculture and agribusiness. Nonetheless, its 200,000 members pale in comparison to Farm Bureau's 6 million constituents. Perhaps more importantly, NFU's lobbying budget, at $180,000 in 2021, was only a fraction of the $2.5 million spent by Farm Bureau.

Further Reading: Rosenberg, N. A., and B. W. Stucki. "The Butz Stops Here: Why the Food Movement Needs to Rethink Agricultural History." *Journal of Food Law & Policy* 13, no. 1 (2018). https://scholar works.uark.edu/jflp/vol13/iss1/7.

October 17, 1955
The Term *Agribusiness* Enters the English Language

Former US Assistant Secretary of Agriculture John H. Davis stood up during the 1955 Boston Conference on Distribution and asserted that modern agriculture was "inseparable" from corporate firms that manufacture farming goods. In coining the word *agribusiness*, he gave a name to an entity whose interests supplanted those of the family farm and would dominate American farming from thereon out.

In *Willard Cochrane and the American Family Farm*, economist Dr. Richard A. Levins suggests that the "shortest possible economic history of U.S. agriculture during the twentieth century would be this: nonfarmers learning how to make money from farming." Companies like John Deere, Cargill, Monsanto, and Pioneer, as well as plenty of other megafirms, began to acquire substantial power in the food system during the fever of agricultural expansion in the seventies. When overproduction created low farmgate prices, these firms continued to grow, even during the crisis for grain farmers in the eighties and the exodus of dairy farms at the turn of the century.

The rise of agribusiness frequently resulted in a loss of independence for the family farm, the terms by which farmers could produce or sell their product now being dictated to them. More importantly, however, the countervailing agency, or market power, of the farmer in the producer–manufacturer–retailer relationship tilted decidedly out of their favor. Lost in the shadows of multinationals, farmers did not have the ability to protect their interests. With such influence behind them, agribusiness firms could largely control the narrative, claiming themselves to be the repository of American values and to be creating technology necessary to feed the world. But in reality, they were instrumental in keeping farmgate prices low, increasing the costs in farming to levels small farmers sometimes couldn't afford, and expediting the shift to corporate agriculture in the United States.

Further Reading: Hamilton, Shane. "Agribusiness, the Family Farm, and the Politics of Technological Determinism in the Post–World War

II United States." *Technology and Culture* 55, no. 3 (2014): 560–90.
http://www.jstor.org/stable/24468434.

May 21, 1963
Farmers Vote against Supply Control in Wheat Referendum

In 1958, Willard Cochrane published his seminal book *Farm Price: Myth and Reality*. He was one of the first major figures in the United States to realize that the free market system cannot work in agriculture, neither in theory nor in practice. More importantly, in this book he delivered his productivist treadmill theory, which predicted what would become of US agriculture: as farmers expand, the supply increases and farmgate prices drop, encouraging farmers to produce more to compensate for lower margins, further depressing prices in a negative feedback loop. He also warned about the rise of agribusiness and the consequences it would have for farmers.

Cochrane eventually found himself advising John F. Kennedy on agricultural matters and then working for him after the 1960 presidential election. With Kennedy's support, Cochrane drafted ambitious legislation proposing supply control for dairy, feed grains, and wheat. He explained how a quota system would lead to higher and more stable profits, as well as less government expenditure in agriculture. Predictably, Cochrane's opponents called him a communist and "killer of freedom," and many farming journals echoed those claims. In 1961, Cochrane's attempt to gain support from both Congress and farmers for supply control had failed.

The Kennedy administration's next attempt was the Agricultural Act of 1962. Most of it got stripped away by Congress. The only measure of supply control that remained open to vote was the wheat quota, which had to be approved by a farmer referendum. The referendum required two-thirds of wheat farmers to accept the legislation. While the bill only addressed one agricultural industry, it was a chance to enact supply control in that sector and prove that it worked, hopefully allowing it to gain traction as an American idea. Opposing them was Farm Bureau, once again looking out for the interests of large agriculture. Dr. Richard A. Levins, biographer of Cochrane, declared the wheat referendum to be the last serious attempt to save the family farm.

The vote resoundingly failed.

Cochrane soon resigned from his post in Washington, being told by detractors to "go back to Khrushchev." He found himself informally blacklisted, with an offer of a prestigious Regents Professorship rescinded. Instead, he returned to teaching economics as a normally tenured professor, spending the rest of his life watching everything he predicted for American agriculture come true.

Further Reading: Levins, Richard A. *Willard Cochrane and the American Family Farm*. Lincoln, NE: University of Nebraska Press, 2000. Print.

December 2, 1971
Earl Butz Is Sworn in as US Secretary of Agriculture

On the whole, Earl Butz gets too much credit for turning American agriculture towards industrialization. His doctrine of large agriculture without price supports had already been advocated by Ezra Taft Benson, the secretary of agriculture under Eisenhower, and for whom Butz served as assistant secretary of agriculture. Nonetheless, the reception each man's ideas received, and therefore the platforms they had to proselytize from, were not the same. Benson's drive to remove government support from agriculture was seen as political suicide at the time and made him an unpopular figure, costing his party votes. Eisenhower emphasized caution, and that if price supports were to be removed, it must be done gradually and tactfully.

Under Nixon, however, Butz was under no restraints while promoting large-scale farming and the values of agribusiness. Owing to high grain prices in the 1970s, when he said that price supports and paying farmers not to plant crops were senseless, farmers believed him. With farmers heeding his infamous call to "plant fencerow to fencerow" and to "get big or get out," he encouraged a mentality of mass agricultural production that permanently changed the country's relationship to farming. In the end, America became a nation of cheap food, made at the expense of the producer.

Further Reading: Thompson, Paul B. "Of Cabbages and Kings." *Public Affairs Quarterly* 2, no. 1 (1988): 69–87. http://www.jstor.org/stable /40435669.

November 29, 1983
The National Dairy Checkoff Program Is Authorized

Although the dairy checkoff program was initiated to be a voluntary payment made by farmers to support the marketing of dairy products, it is now mandatory for dairy farmers to tithe 15¢ per hundredweight of milk produced. On average, that equates to a yearly sum of $34 per cow, or $3,400 per year for a one-hundred cow dairy farm.

The intent of the checkoff program was to fund marketing ventures that enhance the national demand for milk. While the consumption of milk has increased in the US since 1983, the program has come under fire for not only being a financial burden to farmers already dealing with tight margins, but also for various controversies surrounding it. Executives of the program average a salary of nearly $1 million per year, with Tom Gallagher, the CEO, receiving more than $2.6 million in 2021. The program has been accused of a lack of transparency, and at one point, despite being required to do so by Congress, it had not submitted annual financial reports for five years. Finally, most of the checkoff money ends up in the hands of lobbying groups, corporations, and companies that are "big ag friendly," ultimately to the detriment of the family farm. For example, chains like McDonald's and Pizza Hut are often paid millions of dollars by the program to bring out products that contain more milk, financially supporting megafirms that already use their purchasing power to reduce what they pay for dairy products. Alternatively, if not for the dairy checkoff program, the one hundred–cow farmer who milked for thirty years would have $102,000 in retirement savings if he/she were allowed to keep the 15¢ per hundredweight.

Further Reading: Frerick, Austin. *Barons: Money, Power, and the Corruption of America's Food Industry*. Washington, DC: Island Press, 2024. Print.

1995
The Founding of the US Dairy Export Council (USDEC)

Establishing a body to promote overseas market opportunities for American dairy products seemed like an action that could only benefit farmers, allowing them to access broader demand for their milk. However, the rise of the United States as one of the world's top exporters of dairy products pitted the farmer's needs against those far more powerful.

The Dairy Export Incentive Program (DEIP) was established in 1985; exporters were paid to sell American dairy products abroad to make those goods more competitive on the world market. The US Dairy Export Council (USDEC) was founded ten years later to further that intention. However, it wasn't until the early 2000s that the United States aggressively sought international markets for milk products. The North American Free Trade Agreement (NAFTA) opened up commerce with Mexico, Australia was suffering from a drought, and the price of producing milk had risen in New Zealand. All of this helped US dairy exports to increase eight times over in the first two decades of the twenty-first century.

The USDEC receives most of its funding from farmers by means of the dairy checkoff program that they are obligated to pay into. The US government cut back price support programs that had been in place for over fifty years to make American dairy products more competitive internationally, hailing the change as a solution to "soak up" extra production. However, exporters benefit from a low milk price. They were incentivized to lobby for favorable policies and to fund farming journals that encouraged expansion and overproduction, as well as any other way the American domestic market could keep milk cheap. Agribusiness made billions in the first two decades of the twentieth century while, according to Food & Water Watch, the average dairy farm only made a profit in 2006 and 2014. Replacing price supports with a reliance on exports not only privileged corporate priorities but set them against those of the farmer. In 2021, exports rose 10 percent, reaching $7.8 billion in value, while American dairy farmers lost $1.60 for every 100 pounds of milk they made. The numbers from most years tell a similar story.

Further Reading: Food & Water Watch. "The Economic Cost of Food Monopolies: The Dirty Dairy Racket." January 2023. https://www.food andwaterwatch.org/wp-content/uploads/2023/01/RPT2_2301_Econom icCostofDairy-WEB.pdf.

April 4, 1996
The Signing of 1996 Farm Bill
For nearly half a century, the US government sought to reduce farmgate price volatility by taking actions to decrease supply when overproduction depressed farmers' income. For dairy farming, this came in the form of the Milk Price Support Program, where the USDA's Commodity Credit Corporation (CCC) bought and stored excess cheese, butter, and nonfat dry milk to be sold or donated later. While far less active than the milk

quotas practiced in Canada and, until recently, the European Union, it did help guarantee a base price for milk.

Looking to negotiate more access to foreign markets by removing subsidies, policymakers behind the 1996 Farm Bill, also called the Federal Agriculture Improvement and Reform (FAIR) or "Freedom to Farm" Act, removed the milk support structures. The bill also terminated "set-aside programs" that encouraged crop farmers to take land out of production, as well as other regulatory measures meant to limit excess production. While previous farm bills had reduced the government's involvement in domestic agricultural markets, the 1996 Farm Bill represented a full divorce from the concept of supply management. The result was that farmgate prices grew increasingly unstable and were dictated by a deregulated market that disadvantaged the farmer.

In total, the attempt to entirely kill dairy supports with the 1996 Farm Bill was not successful. Backlash led to the 2002 Farm Bill establishing a price support floor of $9.90 per hundredweight, as well as the authorization of the Milk Income Loss Contract (MILC) program until 2012, which favored smaller producers (as will be addressed later). In 2012, however, the MILC program was replaced by the Margin Protection Program (and later the Margin Coverage Program), which requires farmers to pay a premium to receive milk price supports on anything beyond the free "catastrophic" coverage. While some see the initiative as a reasonable compromise between the intentions of the 1996 Farm Bill and the ability of farms to survive low farmgate prices, the cost of the insurance is harder to bear by smaller farms. It can be argued that the ethos of the 1996 Farm Bill, removing government support from the pricing of milk, is very much alive in policymaking.

Further Reading: Alston, Julian M., and Daniel A. Sumner. "Perspectives on Farm Policy Reform." *Journal of Agricultural and Resource Economics* 32, no. 1 (2007): 1–19. http://www.jstor.org/stable/40987348.

January 1, 1998
Dairy Farmers of America Is Founded

As already mentioned, there may be no greater contradiction in the American dairy industry than the co-op Dairy Farmers of America. They have earned their nickname "the milk mafia." Few other organizations in the world have likely been sued as regularly by the people they claim to represent.

In 2008, DFA was found guilty of manipulating cheese prices on the Chicago Mercantile Exchange; in 2013, they settled for a $140 million penalty for artificially lowering milk prices in the Southeast; in 2014, they had to pay an additional $350 million for price fixing; in 2016, the co-op paid $50 million to a group of its member farmers for illegal conspiracy to restrain competition and price fixing in the Northeast; in 2020, after purchasing Dean Foods, the largest food processor in America, DFA was sued over anticompetitive practices. DFA also went to court for price-fixing allegations in 2022, once from producers in the Southwest and once from those in the Northeast.

Since DFA has swallowed or forced out most other cooperatives, most farmers have little choice but to join the co-op if they want to receive a milk check, even as the co-op unabashedly works against their interests.

Further Reading: Kardashian, Kirk. *Milk Money: Cash, Cows, and the Death of the American Farm.* Durham, NH: University of New Hampshire Press, 2012. Print.

2004

The Connecticut Fair Milk Pricing Law Fails to be Adopted

Having grown up on a family dairy farm, Dr. Ron W. Cotterill was one of the few economists who actively tried to make milk's farmgate pricing more favorable to farmers. Working from the Food Marketing Policy Center at the University of Connecticut, he was in a state that is home to small dairy farms disproportionately affected by low milk prices and industry consolidation.

One of Dr. Cotterill's principal initiatives was to convince Connecticut to pass a more just milk pricing law. Based on the "Farmer and Consumer Fair Share Approach" that he proposed with his PhD student Adam Rabinowitz, Cotterill sought to ensure that the retailer's profit on a gallon of milk was proportionate to that of the producer. In other words, grocery stores wouldn't be able to raise the price they charged for milk without sharing the increased earnings with the farmer. Because only 40 percent of milk produced at the time was sold as fluid milk, the bill wouldn't guarantee a complete base price to farmers in Connecticut. However, it would increase their milk checks, help protect the consumer from price gouging, and ensure that retailers didn't soak up the lion's share of profit in the food chain. Perhaps most significant of all, passing this type of milk pricing legislation in Connecticut would create a precedent for other states to follow, as well as prove that the farmer's and consumer's interests can be prioritized over those of powerful retailing firms and manufacturers. In short, it would have provided a blueprint to challenge corporate power in the agricultural sector.

Nonetheless, Cotterill found that there was little appetite to take on the retailers in Connecticut, and after several attempts, the bill quietly died.

Further Reading: Cotterill, Ronald. "A Law to Promote Efficient and Fair Pricing of Milk in Connecticut." No. 1585-2016-134137. Storrs, CT: Food Marketing Center, University of Connecticut, 2003. https://are .uconn.edu/wp-content/uploads/sites/2327/2020/03/CT-Law-to-Promote-Efficient-Fair-Pricing-of-Milk.pdf.

January 31, 2005
The EPA Announces the Air Consent Agreement

Under President George W. Bush, the Environmental Protection Agency (EPA) secretly negotiated with the National Pork Producers Council to reach a deal on enforcing air pollution legislation against farmers. The result was the Air Consent Agreement. It allowed farmers amnesty from the Clean Air Act and other similar regulations in exchange for a small fee that helped fund an emission study by the EPA. The EPA estimated that the 14,000 operations across all sectors that signed up for the program made up 90 percent of factory farms at that time. The exemption was meant to last three and a half years and provide time for the EPA to devise more precise air emissions estimating methodologies (EEMs). With the Biden administration, the exemption had been extended through three additional presidencies.

Large concentrations of confined animals can harm the health of those living near them. The breakdown of manure creates pollutants such as ammonia, methane, nitrous oxide, hydrogen sulfide, particulate matter (PM), and volatile organic compounds (VOCs). In small quantities, these contaminates have little observable effect. In large doses, however, in places such as the San Joaquin Valley in California, they can lead to respiratory problems that include chronic bronchitis, asthma, and in some cases, death.

The quiet protection offered to these large farms further exemplifies the American government's desire for cheap food, even in the face of tangible adverse consequences. Since the signing of the Air Consent Agreement, many states that traditionally house large dairy farms have become increasingly lax on the environmental regulation they impose. In December 2008, the EPA removed federal rules requiring ammonia emissions to be reported by animal feeding operations. In 2018, the EPA denied a request by environmental organizations to once again include mandates to regulate ammonia on large farms.

Further Reading: Wilson, Sarah C. "Hogwash! Why Industrial Animal Agriculture Is Not beyond the Scope of Clean Air Act Regulation." *Pace Environmental Law Review* 24 (2007): 439. https://nationalaglawcenter

.org/publication/comment-hogwash-why-industrial-animal-agriculture
-is-not-beyond-the-scope-of-clean-air-act-regulation-24-pace-environ
mental-l-rev-439-477-2007/.

June 18, 2008
2008 Farm Bill Signed without Hard Cap on Subsidies
The debate on US farm subsidies is contentious and marked by differ-
ing viewpoints, most of them well-intentioned. Some declare they are
necessary to help small farmers, others say they're killing them, while
perhaps the most prudent point out that they distract from a more
important conversation, which is how to restructure US agriculture to
make it sustainable. Regardless, most agree that large farms shouldn't
receive the majority of what is dispersed. However, that has been difficult to prevent.

In 2007, Senators Byron Dorgan and Chuck Grassley reintroduced legislation to put a "hard cap" of $250,000 on annual program payments to
farms. It was meant to close the loophole that allowed large farms to register
their operation as multiple smaller units under different individuals and collect the sum multiple times. The proposal overwhelmingly passed in Congress and was supported by the public. However, the hard cap was dropped
during the final negotiations of the farm bill. The same thing happened in
2014 and 2018, and to date there is still no limit on the subsidies that large
farms can receive. While there is no record of what happened behind closed
doors, many suspect that lawmakers were swayed by lobbyists representing
large farmers.

Although the subsidy payment limit was largely focused on crops, per-
sistent loopholes affected family dairy farms in several ways. Dairy farms
grow a substantial amount of grain and forage to feed cattle, and therefore
large operations rather than small producers reaped the benefits of the subsidy. It also made the public mistrust subsidy support for American farmers,
which eventually affects policymakers' political capital. Finally, the failure to

pass a hard cap on crop subsidies likely took away momentum for attempting something similar for dairy farmers.

Further Reading: Bruckner, Traci. "Agricultural Subsidies and Farm Consolidation." *American Journal of Economics and Sociology* 75, no. 3 (2016): 623–48. https://www.jstor.org/stable/45129315.

September 30, 2012
Expiration of the Milk Income Loss Contract (MILC) Program
The Milk Income Loss Contract (MILC) program was predated by the Northeast Dairy Compact, which itself was a response to attempts to remove milk price supports from the 1996 Farm Bill. The Northeast Dairy Compact was an agreement among six New England states to pay dairy farmers at least $16.94 per hundredweight on milk being consumed as a fluid. The compact met opposition from Upper Midwest politicians, however, particularly in Wisconsin, and the compact was not renewed past 2001.

MILC payments replaced the compact. When the Boston fluid milk price fell below $16.94 per hundredweight, every dairy farmer in the United States was eligible to receive an additional payment of 45 percent of the difference between $16.94 and the Boston price. Because only a portion of milk produced is sold as fluid milk—and the percentage decreased after the turn of the century—a farmer's total milk check was seldom as high as $16.94 per hundredweight. However, it did provide additional income during times of low prices. More importantly, the subsidy allotted to a farm was capped. Farmers could only receive the higher price on the first 2.4 million pounds of annual production, or roughly the equivalent of what 130 cows would produce per year. Therefore, the MILC program was one of the few, and to date, last, subsidy programs that favored smaller farmers over bigger operations. When it was not renewed, it was clear that the family dairy farm did not have the lobbying power of its larger counterpart.

Further Reading: Eberle, Phillip, Darren Moody, Matthew C. Rendleman, and William Peterson. (2005). "Investment Analysis of Alternative Dairy Systems under MILC." Southern Agricultural Economics Association, 2005 Annual Meeting, February 5–9, 2005, Little Rock, Arkansas. https://www.researchgate.net/publication/23515364_Invest ment_Analysis_of_Alternative_Dairy_Systems_under_MILC.

Acknowledgments

Writing this book was hard. Most people, if not all, have something that haunts them. However, knowing that wasn't of any use. It was challenging to go back to the past in order to reconcile what happened to our family, which is mostly to say, to process what it means to not be living on a farm now. When my father passed away, what was difficult suddenly seemed impossible.

I wasn't stuck, but the wheels turned slow enough to make it feel like that. Returning to this book every day meant being reminded over and over again that my father had died, and there were times that made me an unhappy person. My wife, Alessandra, bore the brunt of that. Other people would have lost patience. After five years, other partners might have insisted that I get a full-time job instead of piecing together just enough freelance work to pay half the rent. Instead, she was supportive. She let me lean on her when I needed to. She knew it was a story I had to tell, and she knew why. She has a resilience that I admire, and one that I try to emulate.

My family was kind and invested in helping me explore our past. Together, we joined fragments to make a fuller picture than we had before. That alone made it a fulfilling project. It wasn't easy for them to go back in their minds, either, and think about the things I asked them to, but they did. More importantly, they accepted that I was never going to get their part of the story exactly right. Thank you to my mother, Lorri Dennis; my sister, Whitney Dennis; my aunt, Kelly Atherton; and my late father, Rick Dennis.

I'm grateful for the friends I have. They helped me out in different ways, sometimes not realizing it. They knew when to ask about the book, and when not to. Some of them gave me the odd job at their family companies when they could, if only so I wasn't a complete burden to my wife. Kennys Bookshop in Galway, Ireland, has stood their ground against Amazon and other corporate giants in the book industry, and for over eighty years has supported authors in a way that is as admirable as it is generous. The Kennys family has kept this writer off the streets more than once.

Reading someone's unpublished work is an act of kindness that shows character. These people read the manuscript, in full to offer suggestions, or in part to monitor accuracy: Adrian Frazier, Tristan Burke, Christopher Boon, Martin Keaveney, Eleanor Henderson, Greg Goodell, Jeff Rohalla, Lydia Donnelly, and Jackie Boerman.

Thanks to Jon Fisher for allowing me to throw shade at his cat. I'm sorry that I had to cut that part out of the book, but allow me to memorialize Beatrice here. I can't say that I liked your cat, Jon, but I respected her.

I have much respect and awe for Dr. Richard A. Levins and Dr. Ron Cotterill, not only for the policy information they provided, but for the work they did throughout their lives in trying to address a system that did not favor the family farm. They're my type of heroes. In the same way, I am glad for the time that Pete Hardin, editor of *The Milkweed*, volunteered in letting me pick his brain. His journalism has served the American family dairy farm for a long time.

Some things were true while writing this book that weren't accurate by the time it was published. I describe Canaseraga as a town at its end. For years, that felt like a fact. However, the last few times I went back it seemed like there was a different energy to it. There's now a flea market that brings people out on the weekend and a café that serves gourmet plates that would rival the best in any city. The café is always full, for that reason, and because it is a place where people can find each other and be a community. Tom Capwell still makes a chicken wing pizza in his grocery store that is the best a person can get. Canaseraga is a town that is doing more than persisting, and one that has always been good to my family. I hope they still consider me one of their own.

And another amendment: my cousins have started fly-fishing. I'm not the only one in the family with waders anymore. They take me out to the river when I am home, and the time in the water with them means a lot to me.

Island Press has been an exemplary partner in this project. They put in the hard work to prepare the book for readers and respected its vision the entire way. I owe my editor, Emily Turner, something big and expensive, although I can't think of what could possibly compensate her for her patience. I also have awe and appreciation for the thorough copyediting work of Mike Fleming.

Thanks to Arts Council Ireland for financial support in writing this book.

And thanks to every family that was ever on a dairy farm in the United States. You deserved more than you got. It's important that everyone knows this.

About the Author

Ryan Dennis grew up on a New York dairy farm. Since 2011 he has written the *The Milk House*, a column that has appeared in print agricultural journals in four countries, including *Progressive Dairy* and *Farm and Livestock Directory* in the United States. His debut novel, *The Beasts They Turned Away*, was longlisted for the Republic of Consciousness Prize. He is also the editor of the literary journal *The Milk House*, which features writing on rural subjects.

Photo by Andreas Riemenschneider